Potters of C

Shaping the

Viv Rumbold

**photography by
Val Corbett**

ACKNOWLEDGEMENTS

Arne, help support and encouragement; Janet Baker, historical advice; Maggie Berkowitz, historical advice; Gordon Cameron; Catherine Cannon, graphics; John and Marion Drinkwater, the foreword; Harry Fancy, historical advice; Gordon Fox, historical advice and use of Ambleside Studio Pottery sign; Viv Marston, proof reading; Rene Roberts, dialect poetry

First published in the United Kingdom in 1993 by Midnight Oil, Chapel Yat, Helton, Penrith Cumbria.

The contents of this publication are believed correct at time of printing. Nevertheless the Publishers cannot accept responsibility for errors and omissions or for changes in details given.

ISBN 0 9521428 0 5

©   Viv Rumbold 1993
Val Corbett 1993

Printed by Airey & Stephenson Limited, Penrith, Cumbria

CONTENTS

Foreword

by John Drinkwater

In the last forty years pottery has become a major subject in art colleges and students have been encouraged to explore all the possibilities of the medium. Increasing speed and ease of travel and knowledge gained from books magazines and television have made students aware of pottery from other parts of the world, and museums make the work of past civilisations available to everyone. Recent pottery naturally reflects a greater diversity of influence than ever before. Some college courses provide a thorough practical training in basic skills and technology for students with a clear intention of setting up potteries to provide high quality functional pottery. Other courses give students the technological background they need but encourage innovation. They challenge the traditional boundaries of what can, or what should be done with clay. Non-functional ceramics has helped to blur the artificial distinction between art and craft. There cannot be many people left who believe that painting and sculpture are art, and pottery is something different and inferior called craft.

There was a period in the 1960s and 1970s when the Romantic Idea of escaping from urban pressures to become a poor craftsman in idyllic rural surroundings was very attractive to the young. At first they were able to sell their pots to a public that felt it was buying a part of the rural fantasy. It could not last. Many of the potters were more interested in escaping from the city and living in the country than in making pots. The customers who at first would buy anything hand-made became more discriminating. Life grew harder for the potter. When winter came there were fewer tourists to buy their pots, ice formed on the clay bin and the skin began to wear off the ends of fingers. Only the few for whom the pots were more important than the life-style persisted. Several periods of economic austerity and a still more selective public have ensured that only potters with a serious commitment survive.

Despite the many good art college pottery courses many people decide to become potters without much formal training. Often they have already embarked upon one career before becoming caught up in the fascination of clay. They may have met an inspiring teacher and caught the first wave of enthusiasm, but soon they need no further encouragement; they read every book they can find on the subject and start sending for catalogues of materials and equipment. Probably they will buy a kiln and adapt part of their home as a workshop. They will find that their new obsession is interfering with their career and then that the career is getting in the way of the pottery. At this stage they will start to reorganise their lives so that they can give all their attention to the flood of exciting pottery ideas that is building up in their minds.

For much of the time potters work in isolation or with one or two partners, but when they do meet other potters they naturally talk about their work. A group of Cumbrian potters once had regular meetings in Penrith. At first there was an invited speaker at each meeting, but it was soon realised that potters had so much to say to each other that the speaker was not needed. They went on talking until the caretaker ushered them out. They walked back to their cars still talking and late into the night a small group still stood in a circle in the middle of an almost empty car park talking about kilns. Those of us who are largely self-taught will have learnt the rudiments of firing by a long process of firing a kiln in different ways and carefully examining the charred remains of the pots. The paths of my garden are composed entirely of the firing failures of the past fifteen years. Often we were saved from despair by the knowledge that when we meet a technical problem we can usually find another potter who may have found the solution after a long and expensive search but will be pleased to be able to help us. Very few potters have "trade secrets"; most of us are glad to share what we have learned.

Potters have to make a living in order to continue to make pots, but the primary aim is not to make money - if it was then we would surely find an easier way. We work very hard because we want to. It is after all what many of us gave up other careers to do. The chief frustration is in having to stop; to fill in tax forms, mend the roof or take a holiday. Ceramics is a huge subject; each of us can only understand a small part of it in one lifetime. Success lies in finding the area that suits us best, spending the rest of our life exploring it and producing work which changes and gets better from year to year. We are self-motivated; we set ourselves goals that stretch our imaginations and develop our sensitivity to the innate qualities of the materials that we use. We know when we make progress and we know when we fail, but the customer also has a say in our success or failure. If she does not buy our pots we fail and have to give up. If we stop exploring, settle for a small range of products that we know can sell and keep reproducing them mechanically, whatever anyone else thinks, we know we have failed. This is a dilemma that we all have to face and it imposes a discipline that, on the whole, is good for us. We only succeed if we produce work which at the same time satisfies our creative aspirations and is valued by the customer. This keeps us in contact with the real world.

It is difficult to generalise about potters, who are essentially individualists. I have tried to do so but I am afraid that there will be some who do not recognise themselves in what I have written. The work is physically exacting but we are fortunate in being able to follow our chosen course. Many people wear themselves out doing jobs they do not want to do. So many of us suffer physically as a result of our work that there ought to be a recognised disease called "Potter's back", but potters never willingly stop being potters. Some of us have rather grandiose ideas about what we are trying to do, but what it really boils down to is this; that once we have got to know the feel and smell of clay we can't leave it alone; we are addicted.

Historical map of past areas of pottery making in Cumbria

Carlisle and Wigton areas
Mid - late 19th century

Pipes (tobacco)
Firebrick and sanitary pipes
Red bricks and tiles

Hadrian's Wall

Brampton and Carlisle area

Roman Pottery
A.D.43 - 5th century

First Blackburnished ware
Later Knapton
and Huntcliffe wares

● Brampton

● Carlisle

Huntcliffe cooking pot

● Wigton

● Penrith

Wetheriggs Pottery

1855 - present day

Decorative slip - trailed
earthenware and gardenware

Beehive Kiln now scheduled Industrial Monument

Tobacco

● Maryport

● Cockermouth

Into Whitehaven
Port

● Workington

Rum

West Cumbria Coal and Clay Resources
Many coarseware potteries in West Cumbria from 17th century
Later quality ware produced in the
"Gins" area and other areas
Made and exported up until 1915 (approx)

Whitehaven ●

● Egremont

Flintmill

Flint ground and "burned" at Egremont (flints came from
Thames and north of Ireland,
used to strengthen bodies and in glazing)

3 bottle kilns at
Whitehaven pottery factory

YORKSHIRE DALES

● Burton - in - Lonsdale
Important pottery area from 1750-1945
Early - coarse black and brown ware
Mid - decorative earthenware
From 1840-1945 Stoneware jars and
bottles etc., and later firebricks

Stone bottles used for Irish whisky

A Brief History Of Past Pottery-Making Sites In Cumbria

Following Bronze Age, Iron Age and Roman pottery, Cumbria does not appear to have produced pottery again until much later. However over in Yorkshire, some wares were made during the Saxo-Norman and mediæval periods. The two areas of importance were around Whitehaven in West Cumbria from the 17th century, and from 1855 at Wetheriggs near Penrith. They were sited on deposits of clay, but there was also coal in West Cumbria. Close by, just half a mile from the Cumbrian border was a third area of importance, Burton-in-Lonsdale in the Yorkshire Dales. "Black Burton" was rich in coal and red pot clay. Stoneware clay and a coarser fireclay were found later under the coal seams.

Pre-Roman
Pottery was made in the county during the Bronze and Iron Ages, and examples of artefacts can be seen in Tullie House Museum, Carlisle.

Romans: AD 43 to the fifth century
When the Romans invaded Britain in AD 43 they found some potteries existing in the south and south-east. They brought their own pottery with them and began to set up pottery production units varying from small workshops to major industrial organisations. Due to military contracts, such production was started at Brampton to supply the soldiers along Hadrian's Wall and surrounding areas. There were hand-made black burnished pots and crude grey pots (with calcite grit) known as Knapton ware. These were burned - a crude method of firing - on a bonfire. Later, they made wheel-thrown greyish types of cooking pots, called Huntcliffe ware, which were probably fired in kilns. There was also a Roman tilery at Eskdale, and examples can be seen in Whitehaven Museum. The Roman era of pottery ended in the fifth century when England was divided into self-governing communities.

Post Mediæval: 1650 to 1800

THE BURTON IN LONSDALE POTTERIES (1750 TO 1945)
Burton-in-Lonsdale, near Ingleton, had the natural resources and became a very important pottery making area. Many potteries sprang up around the River Greta and began producing at first black and brown wares and then later slip-trailed earthenware, some of which was highly ornamental. Each country pottery had its speciality. One of Burton's was the Puzzle Jug. These jugs have a hollow rim with protruding spouts, and the hollow handle is also joined into the rim. They cut out designs around the neck and a humorous verse was then trailed in slip around the barrel of the jug. The most popular rhyme at Burton was:

> Gentlemen now try your skill
> I'll hold you sixpence if you will,
> That you don't drink unless you spill.

The challenge was to drink beer without spilling, and resulted in endless fun and wagers.

Some names of pottery families in Burton include Baggaley, Bateson, Walmsley and Seward. From 1840, stoneware was also produced at Baggaley Pottery in two kilns, one for earthenware the other for stoneware. They made stoneware, jars and bottles, some bottles being supplied to Ireland for the whiskey distilleries. Later on, firebricks were also produced. All potteries had ceased production by 1945. Examples of Burton ware can be seen at the Museum of North Craven Life at Settle.

WEST CUMBERLAND POTTERIES 1637 TO 1915

The first recorded potters in West Cumberland come from entries in Bridekirk parish church at Little Broughton. Thomas Foorth of Dearham, near Maryport was potting in 1637. In 1790 a pottery was being operated at Dearham by John Coulthard. Later his son John was making yellow ware dishes and puzzle jugs with chocolate ornamentation until the early nineteenth century. Pottery was being made throughout the eighteenth century and well into the nineteenth in several potteries at Little Broughton.

Materials were abundantly available on site in West Cumberland. Road transport was however far from good, and later wares were exported by sea. In 1845, the Maryport to Carlisle railway opened. This was extended to Whitehaven in 1847, making the area more accessible.

King Charles II in 1674 had granted the mineral rights to the Lowther family of Westmorland. Sir John Lowther wished to exploit these resources and engaged a brick-maker, Edward Gibson. By 1686 Mr Gibson was very successfully producing a large volume of bricks and tiles. Sir John was already exporting coal to Ireland in large quantities. When he discovered that the Irish bought in Dutch tiles, he tried to gain this market for his own product. He felt sure there were also opportunities for earthenware manufacture. Jeremy Lyons, a potter from Liverpool came to Whitehaven in 1687 to start a new pottery, but he encountered problems with the coal and eventually left.

Aaron Wedgwood of Burslem, son of Thomas, came in 1698 at Sir John's request to make the fine red ware that was being produced in Staffordshire at that time. However the local coal caked and Aaron was unsuccessful. In spite of this he decided to stay and went to live near Dearham, when he married Margaret Tunstall. By 1708 he had a successful pottery business at Whistling Syke on the nearby moors. He died in 1741 and three of his sons became potters at Rebton.

Whitehaven was becoming a very important port. By the mid eighteenth century it was a boom town and its port was the third most important in the British Isles. Tobacco had been imported for many years from Virginia and rum from the West Indies. Sir John Lowther had two pipehouses built in 1698 for the manufacture of clay pipes for the smoking of tobacco. He had managed to find a suitably fine earthenware clay in the area. By 1820 the port was exporting iron ore, coal, linen and earthenware to Canada, the West Indies and South America, in sailing ships built at Whitehaven. Georgian Whitehaven was the first post-Renaissance town to be planned. Many fine houses were built for wealthy merchants and sea captains.

Pipe production continued for many years. In Carlisle there were pipe makers in the late eighteenth century, who also made firebricks and sanitary pipes. Close by at Little Corby, red bricks and tiles were being made. At this time in Wigton there are records of pottery families called Steward, Lowther, Williamson and Young. Crossbarrow pottery near Clifton was successfully operating from the second half of the eighteenth century and continued well into the nineteenth. The Ostles potted for approximately this same period at Dearham. The Marsh Pottery at Workington was run by John and Thomas Dunbar during the last half of the nineteenth century. They made high quality moulded wares known as Rockingham and Cane earthenware. During the early nineteenth century, Fox House Farm Pottery made a yellow quality ware at Broughton Moor.

The Ladypit Pottery, situated at Sunny Hill on the north side of the town, operated in the early eighteenth century and produced Ironstone cane ware, black glazed teapots, porphyry and grave vases.

The Ginns district of Whitehaven was particularly rich in clay and coal and had several potteries.
The Ginns House Pottery (1796 - 1915) initially made coarse brown wares. From 1834 John Kitchen ran the pottery and eventually employed twenty potters who made fine agate wares and even exported. Frederick and John Pateman operated Ginns House until its closure.
The Glass House Pottery, known as the Yellow Pottery, was run by John Tunstall and Joseph Goulding from 1813 to 1915. They made some moulded wares and also exported.

The Whitehaven Pottery (1800 - 1915) The new large and prestigious factory was opened by Peter Woodnorth, and built on the lines of those in Staffordshire. It made mainly white earthenware with a blue and white transfer decoration. John Wilkinson from Burslem took over in 1824 and the pottery eventually employed 180 potters, women, girls and boys. Three bottle kilns were operated for the firings. They used a common white clay from Poole in Dorset, and the debris (china clay) of soft Cornish granite. Flint was obtained from the Thames or the north of Ireland, and burnt and ground at the Egremont Flint Mill. Smalt, made from fusing cobalt oxide, potassium carbonate and silica, was used for blue decoration. Some pots were wheel-thrown and turned on a lathe; others were moulded or slip-cast and then transfers or sprig-moulded decoration added. Lead ore for glazes was brought from the Keswick mine, owned by John Tebay, Wilkinson's partner. Sometimes iron or manganese oxide was added for brown or purple hues. The pots were fired in fire-clay boxes known as saggars, wrapped in straw and placed in hazel crates or baskets for carriage.

Whitehaven Pottery Puzzle Jug

The Whitehaven Pottery never achieved the financial success of the Staffordshire potteries. It could not compete as its costs were higher, even though its products were of an equally high quality, and it closed in 1915. In its heyday, Whitehaven Pottery exported wares and is thought to have supplied the Lowthers in Whitehaven Castle. Its range of goods included: tobacco jars, smokers' outfits, marriage dishes, darning eggs, rum-butter dishes, tureens, candlesticks, bowls, bedroom sets, puzzle jugs, frog mugs, pint mugs and money boxes. There are many examples of these West Cumberland potters wares in the Whitehaven Museum and the Helena Thompson Museum, Workington.

Victorian

WETHERIGGS POTTERY, 1855 TO PRESENT DAY

The pottery was sited on deposits of red clay four miles south-east of Penrith. It was originally built as a brick and tile works on the estate of Brougham and Vaux and adjacent to the Eden Valley branch railway. Coal from West Cumberland was brought by rail for the firings. Ten years later, the Schofields started producing flower pots and domestic glazed farm kitchenware as well.

Slip for decoration was made from ball clay and white clay from Brough Moor. These clays were mixed with water to a creamy consistency, and cobalt or copper oxide was added for blues or greens. A cow's horn, with a protruding goose quill was used for slip trailing.

They used a simple design of feathering, dots and squiggles. This type of decoration, used in country potteries of the time, is thought to have originated in the Netherlands. Their glazes were made from red lead, obtained from Newcastle, ground flint, clay and water. This glaze when fired to about 1080°C produced a pleasing honey-coloured gloss.

Towards the turn of the century, Wetheriggs was competing with cheaper mass-produced, transfer decorated white wares, from Stoke-on-Trent. In their struggle to survive they experimented with more ornamental wares. They also had to compete with another type of pottery. The new Art and Craft movement advocated by people such as William Morris resulted in the birth of ornamental and colourful art pottery studios.

Wetheriggs Salt-Kit, 1887

John Ruskin (1819 - 1900), writer, artist and critic, who lived at Brantwood, Coniston also believed that ".. there was insufficient beauty in life ..". Subsequently, in 1904 his daughter gave permission for his name to be given to such an art pottery studio at Smethwick in the Black Country. There was now a departure from the apprentice learning pottery a trade. Ceramics was introduced into art colleges as both an academic and practical subject and as a formal course of study.

Wetheriggs went through another lean time during the General Strike. After the Second World War, the pottery had become run-down and needed repair. Aids such as diggers for clay and diesel-driven machinery, which was much less labour-intensive than steam were acquired. Some new young potters joined, and with renewed enthusiasm they began exhibiting new decorative and more colourful wares both locally and nationally. After 1960 the pottery again began to fall into disrepair and produced little more than flower pots.

The Schofield family and its descendants, the Thorburns, who had run the pottery until then, finally decided to sell. In 1972 Wetheriggs was bought by an art college trained graphic designer and his wife. Prior to the purchase they were obliged to learn the traditional way of pottery making from Mr Thorburn.

As part of the contract it was also mandatory to continue the Wetheriggs slipware decorated with feathered and trailed designs such as the speciality illustrated. After six months training the Jonathan and Dorothy Snell were allowed to buy the pottery. Hans Ulrich, a potter they had first met at Findhorn in Scotland, joined them for a time. They began renovating the buildings and Dorothy established a weaving shed. In 1973 the Department of the Environment scheduled the pottery as a National Industrial Monument. The Snells built a new shop and cafe and were very successful in making Wetheriggs breathe new life as a tourist destination and art centre. In 1989 the Snells decided to sell, presenting a rare opportunity for someone to buy this unique country pottery. Peter Strong was that person. He was potting at Clapham in the Yorkshire Dales, but had previous associations with Soil Hill Pottery at Halifax, another country pottery that was very run-down and which he wanted to rescue. Peter is an expert on and a collector of English country pottery, and was in the most practical sense, perfectly placed to continue as a manufacturer and exponent of this tradition and continue the remaining restoration work.

Post war

AMBLESIDE STUDIO POTTERY (1947 - 1982)

Ambleside Studio Pottery, located at "The Potter's Wheel", The Old Mill, was an off-shoot of the Art and Craft Movement revival art potteries and the Leach movement. It was run by George Frederick Cook from 1947 to 1968, and by the Jackson family from 1968 to 1982. George was a ceramic philosopher and innovator. On leaving the army in 1945, he trained in ceramics under Dora Billington at the Central School of Art in London. George had been badly injured in the war and had become a Christian Scientist, and his religious beliefs became an important part of his life.

A businessman invited George to come and run his pottery at the Old Mill in Ambleside. Prior to this, George had spent a short time at the Burton-in-Lonsdale Potteries where he had been taught a more simplified throwing technique by Ben Bateson. He subsequently taught this method to his employees.

After a time George became dissatisfied with the arrangements at the Old Mill, and he hired the room underneath to set up his own pottery. To start with he made slipware with *scraffito*, sometimes adding humorous verse. He made tankards, mugs and press-moulded dishes, firing them in an electric kiln.

Later he was able to make reduced stoneware and porcelain, having acquired a vast oil-fired kiln. George had some happy accidents owing to the slow cooling-down cycle of this kiln which resulted in a crystalline development in his black glaze. Fortunately he managed to repeat this and it became one of his standard glazes. As part of his continuing experimentation George tested a variety of ash types in his glazes, including bracken and many other local materials.

George managed eventually to obtain the use of the top floor of the mill. Later he opened a new showroom having much more space and wider range of pottery. Having a designer's eye, George scoured the rest of the country buying other art and craft work to complement his wares. He even imported artefacts including textiles, from Sweden and Italy. This was very avant-garde for the 1950s and the quality of the work for sale rivalled any of the top galleries of the time.

George was a very fair employer and looked after his workers very well. Money was not his main motivator and he was satisfied by covering the costs of the pottery and wages. He put his religious beliefs into practice.

Following her training, Maggie Berkowitz worked in the summer of 1949 in George's studio. Later Gordon Fox worked for him as an apprentice, staying seven years. He remembers George as a very kind and fair person, perhaps a little eccentric and unpredictable, but never boring. Gordon admired him greatly and regards him as an unsung ceramic pioneer, way ahead of his time.

Many students of ceramics from Belfast College of Art were lucky enough to spend six month placements under George's supervision. In 1968 George moved to Ireland where he had many contacts. The pottery was taken over by the Jackson family who continued to make stoneware and hand-painted earthenware using underglaze colours followed by a clear glaze. Success followed the Jacksons for many years. However in 1982, falling profits obliged them to close the pottery. The Old Mill is now a craft and general gift shop.

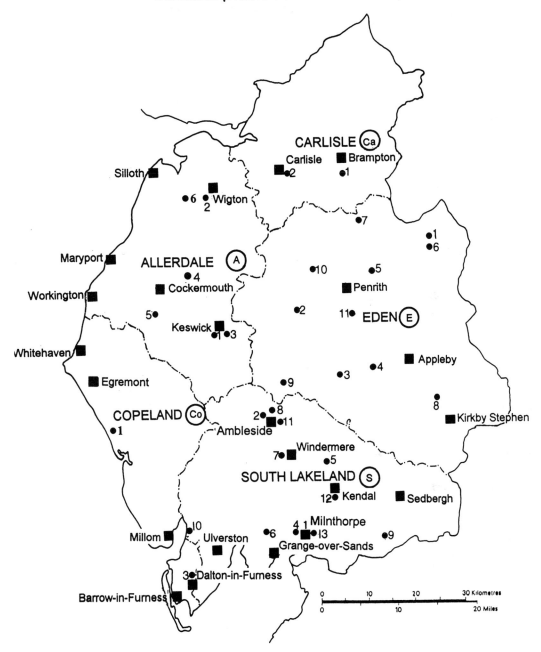

Cumbrian potters and ceramic artists, 1993

CARLISLE (Ca)

Carlisle ●2 ■ Brampton
●1

Silloth ■

●6 ●Wigton
2

●7

●1
●6

ALLERDALE (A)

Maryport ■

●10 ●5

●4
■Cockermouth ■Penrith

Workington ■

5● ●2 11● EDEN (E)

Keswick ■
1● ●3

Whitehaven ■

●4 ■Appleby

Egremont ■ ●3

●9

●8

COPELAND (Co) ●8
2● ■11 ■Kirkby Stephen
●1 Ambleside

7● ■Windermere
●5

SOUTH LAKELAND (S)

12● ■Kendal ■Sedbergh

Millom ■ ●10
Ulverston ■ ●6 4●1 ■Milnthorpe
●13 ●9
3● ■Dalton-in-Furness Grange-over-Sands

Barrow-in-Furness ■

0   10   20   30 Kilometres
0   10   20 Miles

Jane Smith

101 Lake Road, Ambleside, Cumbria LA22 0DB Map code S11
☎ 05394 34038
Workshop open by arrangement to the public.

Jane makes a wonderful range of pottery, and she is probably best known for her beautiful delicate translucent porcelain bowls with carved fish designs. The pale green celadon-type glaze and mother-of-pearl lustre enhance the completed pieces. Her bowls however represent just one aspect of an extremely talented lady.

Detail from porcelain bowl, showing pierced and cut-out design

She fires in an electric kiln where all her pots are biscuited. In the glaze firings she separates the earthenware, fired to only 1080°C, from her porcelain and stoneware which are glaze fired to 1280°C. Lustre-decorated pots are fired for a third time to 780°C. She also has a small raku kiln, that she uses for other things such as little horse figures with white crackle glaze. Jane sells her work in galleries in Cumbria and further afield.

Jane also uses a coarse crank mixture to make large, rangy animals. These cats, tigers, leopards and unicorns often get used as garden ornaments. Her sense of humour is demonstrated by her porcelain dragon and angel-fish teapots, and a series of lampbases comprising groups of acrobats - some in clusters, some head-to-toe, some in pyramids. She has also produced large white earthenware hens with brightly painted decoration. Jane is experimenting further with the use of coloured slips and earthenware, taking advantage of the range of colours that can be obtained at lower maturing temperatures.

Jane at home with two of her tigers

Jane came to ceramics late in life, and is an exceptional example of what can be achieved with a combination of talent and determination. Jane's first ideas of pottery was as a hobby, and she took a leisure course at the Cumbria College of Art and Design in Carlisle. There she was taught by Mary Douglas, at that time head of ceramics. Mary recognised her potential and encouraged Jane to study a vocational HND course as a mature student. This move fitted in well with Jane's desire at that time to find a new direction. Mike Dodd was another of her teachers at Carlisle. She spent part of her placement at Wetheriggs Pottery near Penrith.

Jane's first pottery was set up in the front room of her house in Keswick, deep in bed-and-breakfast country. She met her husband, Andrew Morris, who is a professional photographer and they moved to their present premises in Ambleside. The couple have bought a nearby cottage for renovation.

Alston Pottery

Alston Pottery, Alston, Cumbria CA9 3RP   Map code E1
Open by arrangement

Walter Storey set up a pottery in 1972 in the old brewery adjacent to the route of the Pennine Way. In 1979 he moved out and rented the building to another potter. He returned in 1992 with his daughter, son and son's girl-friend, all three of who are potters. The old brewery complex has many lovely old buildings and offers plenty of scope for them all. They now work separate potteries on the same site sharing some kiln facilities and a showroom that is opened monthly to invited gallery owners. This pottery complex has tremendous potential with the wealth of talent on the site and is a very exciting prospect.

Walter Storey
☎ 0434 381821

Walter installed an oil-fired trolley kiln with a 75 cu ft capacity and from 1972 to 1979 he made oxidised domestic stoneware, selling widely, supplying restaurants and galleries. He decided he needed a change and went to the Hotham Pottery in Putney where for the next ten years he lectured at the adult education centre. Walter is an expert in glaze technology and before his return to the North spent some time in China doing consultancy work for a pottery factory. At present he is converting a barn to use as a glaze laboratory and has built a catenary arch kiln outside for salt glaze.

Walter uses a Fulham's stoneware body clay that produces speckles through his glazes. His choice of glaze colours reflects the rugged Pennine landscape. He fires to 1260°C in an electric kiln at present, but will use the trolley kiln when he has time to increase the volume of work. His pots are thrown and then modified by kinks and tucks. They have elaborate ribbon-like handles and well-defined pouring lips. The glazes are dipped and trailed, sometimes one on top of another. Living beside the South Tyne, he is interested in the swirling flow of water and the relationship between movement and stillness that have influenced his recent designs for decorative indoor ceramic fountains.

Walter studied ceramics under Michael Casson at Harrow College of Art. Casson rigorously selected his students, almost all subsequently become potters. Walter's contemporaries included Jane Hamlyn, Janice Chalenko, Peter Starkey, Susie Cree and Steve Course - all very well-known potters of the present day.

Walter Storey:
Stoneware plate and mug,
photographed in his garden.

Stefan Storey & Caroline Batten
Large earthenware vase

Stefan Storey and Caroline Batten
☎ 0434 382080

Stefan is a very skilled production thrower with an innate sense of form. Most of his pots are on a large scale. Caroline is the expert on decoration. They have a fairly clear division of labour and make pots jointly on this basis. The range of thrown ware includes large colourful jugs with flamboyant pouring lids and extruded fluted handles, platters made oval by a sharp jerk soon after throwing then adorned with curved lugs and twisted extruded feet as well as beautiful large bowls, vases and lampbases.

For the majority of their work, they use a white earthenware, and a red earthenware clay for their terra cotta garden ware The biscuit firing is high - to 1100°C. Decoration starts with a base transparent lead-bisilicate glaze. Colour stained onglaze is next sponge-stencilled, trailed or brushed on achieving striking blues and greens, or pink, peach and purple hues. Caroline creates bold floral designs, although some are sea-inspired. Others have wax-resist areas painted over, then designs scratched through and black commercial stains painted into the lines. The glaze firing is in an electric kiln to 1110°C with a long soak.

Caroline and Stefan are experimenting with hand-made tiles and plan to expand this side of their work. Stefan has made wooden-framed templates into which soft clay is rolled. He runs a wire-cutter along the top that is finally smoothed with a rubber kidney.

Stefan trained for four years at the Dart Pottery in Totnes, Devon where he met Caroline who was training to be a decorator. They were offered temporary jobs in a large pottery in Bermuda with Stefan production throwing whilst Caroline ran the decoration department. Returning to England, they moved to Alston to set up their pottery.

Stefany Storey
☎ 0434 382226

Stefany has spent some of her life in Provence in south-east France. She is in the early stages of her exciting design development. Her love of animals and plants shows in her choice of subjects. She makes a variety of wall plaques including vases of flowers, frogs or lizards. These are painted and glazed in vibrant Mediterranean colours. She also makes a variety of planters, some with integral saucers. Others have sprig-moulded or press-moulded additions or scalloped rims. Stefany enjoys mould making and plans to make more use of them for her standard lines. The clay she has chosen for her work is a white earthenware. Her decoration designs begin with a raised fine outline, trailed in thick slip. This forms a container for the infill of commercially stained underglaze colours that are then trailed or brushed in. The pots are then dipped in a transparent glaze. They are raw-glazed and once-fired in an electric kiln to 1110°C.

Maggie Angus Berkowitz

21-23 Park Road, Milnthorpe, Cumbria LA7 7AD   Map code S1
☎ 05395 63970
Visits by appointment only

Maggie is a ceramic artist who paints on tiles. For her canvas, she uses biscuited blanks or vitrified tiles, glazes and metal oxides as her paint. She initially trails the lay-out or framework of her design, which has many stages and firings through to completion. Most of her work is done to commission, and is usually in the form of a large panel of tiles as a mural or floor. One such example is *The Lion Tamers* an 11' by 5' mural for the Great Ormond Street Hospital for Sick Children. She also takes commissions for work on a smaller scale for kitchens and bathrooms.

Maggie holds a National Diploma in Design from Lancaster School of Art. She also trained as a teacher at the University of London Institute of Education, during which she started to learn about pottery. She became an unofficial technician at the Institute, looking after the firings in the evening. On completing this course she sold some of her work to Heals in order to get her fare home.

Next summer George F Cook offered Maggie a job in his Ambleside pottery. She made three dozen patterned slip-trailed dishes each day, and thus learned to appreciate discipline. She next moved to Brathay Hall in Ambleside, where she taught Art on month-long residential courses to young industrial apprentices. During her two years at Brathay Maggie persuaded her employers that she needed further training in pottery, and they paid for her for three months whilst she studied under Dora Billington at the Central School in London. Then she moved to one of Cambridgeshire's innovative Village Colleges. She also taught pottery at a Teachers' Studio Workshop in Cambridge, and sold her own pottery through the Cambridge Designer Craftsmen's Shop.

Eager for travel, Maggie next went to Italy and spent a summer working in a tile workshop remarkable for its tunnel kiln. She painted tiles and taught English to the daughter of the family she was staying with. Maggie even managed to win a one-year scholarship from the Italian government to study at the Istituto Statale d'Arte per la Ceramica. Tanzania was her next stop, where she taught for a while before moving on to America to study at Columbia University in New York.

Maggie returned to England in 1970 and brought up her four children. She continued to teach Art and Pottery, now at Milnthorpe Secondary School, where she stayed for the next eleven years. Since 1984 she has worked full-time as a ceramic artist, spending three months in 1990 with the Noohi Tile Company of Japan with the help of a travel grant from Northern Arts. Her superb work is exhibited and installed all over the country.

Maggie Berkowitz:
Tile floor installed in Cambridge for David Kindersley.

John Kershaw:
Stoneware bottle form illustrating his decorative handle finish.

John Kershaw

40 Main Street, Windermere, Cumbria LA23 1DY   Map code S7
☎ 05394 44844
Open shop hours

John makes a range of functional stoneware, large bread crocks, storage, jars, large platters and lamp bases. He uses a mixture of smooth stoneware and crank clays. The pots have strong rouletted and incised decoration with matt glazes. He is widely known for these pots and also his range of planters, some of which are slab built with a coarser raku clay. He also makes press-moulded wall-plaques.

More recently he has developed his work in a sculptural direction with less predictable results. John prefers to work directly on the pot and does the minimum amount of turning. He began experiments with surface texture by adding and pressing powdered clay onto a freshly thrown pot - then continuing to throw, thus achieving an immediate encrusted effect. To add another dimension, he will sometimes press on red powdered clay. Decoration is applied immediately, without too many follow-up processes. His handles and lugs have become more ornate. To achieve this he presses clay into old printing blocks then rolls it to form handles. Finally thin coils of clay are twisted or wound round the handles before they are attached to the pot. Some pots with these lovely gnarled handles have their necks deliberately tilted off-centre. Other pots have handles made from plaited coils.

John uses combinations of white slip with oxide-stained slips trailed on, under a dolomite glaze. His most recent glaze, which is very reactive, is based on barium, lithium and copper, producing a deep bluey turquoise alkaline green. After biscuit-firing, thin washes of body stains and glazes are laid on. He has added a tin glaze to his range. This gives a white gloss and feels pleasant to the touch when used on mugs and tea-pots. The glaze firing is to 1260°C in an electric kiln. He also has a small raku kiln and fires jugs and vases producing lovely contrasts of black, crackle-white and turquoise.

John originally trained as a civil engineer and followed this by teaching maths and physics for four years. His deputy head knew of his interest in art and suggested he took a part-time course. The following year he left teaching for a full-time Foundation course at Manchester Polytechnic. Next he studied three-dimensional design and in the final year specialised in ceramics.

John had spent many holidays in the Lake District and in 1972 decided to set up his first pottery and shop in Windermere. He enjoys meeting the people who buy from his shop, and does not find them intrusive. Over half of his sales are direct, the rest through galleries in Cumbria and further afield.

Geoff Barnfather

Briar Cottage, Castle Carrock, Cumbria CA4 9NB   Map code Ca1
☎ 0228 70378
By appointment only

In addition to his full-time post, Geoff has always produced his own work in a variety of materials. Clay, sometimes combined with steel, has been the main medium for the past five years. Pieces may comprise a group which can be stacked or assembled in different ways according to preference. Architectural and organic elements feature strongly, as do archæological remains, disintegrating buildings, garden plants and the environment in general. He makes drawings before the execution of a piece. These are both a starting point and complete in their own right, forming a large part of his work. He extracts from them some of the ideas as a preliminary for a sculpture. These ideas evolve as they are then translated into three-dimensional forms.

Geoff uses buff-coloured raku clay, which withstands thermal shock. In the construction of his pieces he uses mainly basic press-moulds as well as adjustable moulds that he has made from wood and plaster, and may use slabbed additions. He hand-build from small elements. When complete, pieces are slowly dried and biscuit fired with a slow rise in temperature to 1000°C. After this firing, he may brush on oxides, often using raw sienna which produces a range of tones from ochre yellow to dark brown. Geoff next places his pieces on a bed of fire bricks and works on them one at a time, pouring sawdust over them in a deliberate manner. He next uses a welding torch to smoke-fire selected areas. He likes the control that he obtains with this process, as it allows him to vary the shade of blackness and colour of the oxides by the intensity of heat applied. Finally he goes over the whole piece with the torch to strengthen it. Steel parts are welded, and may be painted, and are an integral part of the form, but may also act as a plinth or stand.

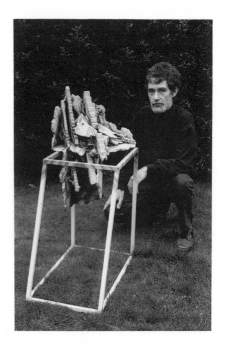

Crank clay sculpture with steel plinth.
Photographed in Geoff's garden.

Geoff studied Fine Art, specialising in sculpture, at St Martin's College, London, followed this with a teacher's certificate course at London University and then taught on a Foundation course in Warwickshire. He then moved to Yorkshire where he was in charge of three-dimensional design and sculpture for students undertaking teacher training at Middleton St George. In 1978 Geoff moved to Cumbria College of Art and Design as head of Three-dimensional Studies and Sculpture. He is currently head of Fine Art, now that a degree course has been validated.

At present, he is moving in another direction in his work, and is drawing subjects relating to water and nature, and expects to use mixed media with some ceramic elements as the ideas grow into sculptures.

Gail Bullock

Skiddaw Pottery, Rear Lake Road, Keswick, Cumbria CA12 5DQ   Map code A1
☎ 07687 74846
Pottery and shop open to public, but confirm by telephoning if coming a long way.

Gail's choice of colours has evolved and been influenced by the Cumbrian landscape. Her slatey greens, greys and browns are reminiscent of the lichens ferns and fungi seen on the fells, rocks and screes. She pays great attention to finish, both to the appearance and function of the pot. Her products are domestic and decorative oxidised stoneware. There is rather more of the latter, many of which are associated with light. She makes fantasy castles, lamp shades and bases, pot pourri and aromatherapy pots, night-light candle holders all with pierced and cut-out designs. Some have texture and modelled additions applied. Gail also produces a range of planters. She has recently begun collecting shells and will introduce their shapes into her planter designs.

She uses a stoneware body, which she mixes with grog and de-airs in a pugmill, then throws on an electric wheel. Turning at the leather-hard stage is an important step in achieving the final shape and creating the foot. At this point she cuts out designs and adds texture or modelling before drying and first firing to 940°C. Larger pieces are thrown on bats and lifted from the wheel-head to avoid distortion. Following the biscuit firing, she brushes on oxides and body stains. She then applies wax-resist to the parts she does not wish to glaze. Gail has several basic glazes, all matt, which she mixes herself. These are applied by dipping and pouring, before the final firing to 1280°C in an electric kiln.

Gail is a Cumbrian, born in Keswick, and has lived here all her life except whilst she was training. She began that on the Arts Foundation Course at Blackpool, then took more O-levels at Carlisle FE College before moving to Kent where she studied vocational crafts (mainly ceramics) at Medway College of Design. She found living in the South very different but she made some good friends. In 1974 Gail moved back to Keswick where she set up her pottery and shop in the town, and where she has lived with her family ever since.

Apart from her own designs, she accepts commissions and has made many sports trophies and other personalised items. She has an international following of visitors who holiday in the area and add to their collections of her work. In her future work she intends to concentrate more on individual designs.

Gail decorating one of her stoneware castles

Geoff and Christine Cox

Cox Ceramics, Stoddah Gate Barn, Penruddock, Nr Penrith, Cumbria CA11 0RY   Map code E2
☎ 07684 83820
Not normally open to visitors, but exceptional arrangements are possible

Geoff is interested in the interplay of textures, light and shade. Chris was once a painter, and her concern is mainly with colour. For most of the time they work independently except for sharing the same stoneware clay and use of kiln. When they do work together it is on standard lines, such as fish forms and dragons' eggs.

Geoff makes tall sculptured clay figures based on a cylinder. They have costumes reminiscent of mediaeval crusaders or Japanese warriors. He is not too concerned with authenticity, more in the evocation of images. To create textured components, Geoff rolls out sheets of clay onto, for example, fabrics and leather. He then cuts the sheets into thin strips which he applies to the main cylinder, building up the structure in layers. He then adds more modelled details, paying particular attention to the elaborate head-dresses. The results are imposing, and seem to possess a dignified air. Some of his figures are female and these he may adorn with wimples or bustles.

Geoff studied three-dimensional design in furniture, ceramics and silversmithing at High Wycombe and followed this with a year's teacher training at Brighton. Chris has a degree in Fine Art from Manchester Art College, and she too underwent teacher training. Thus they met soon after when they both taught Art in a Rochdale school.

Geoff Cox: stoneware figures with textured clay garments

24

Geoff included ceramics in his teaching work, and after their marriage Chris took evening classes where she learned to throw clay. They progressed to having a joint exhibition at Rochdale Municipal Art Gallery. Geoff then took a new post, teaching Art and ceramics at Beverley Grammar School. Chris stayed at home, developing her ideas, experimenting with clay and began to sell her work. She made a gradual transition from thrown pieces of a functional nature to the more abstract, hand-built forms that she produces now.

Christine Cox: filling stoneware planters

Chris' work mainly comprises bowl forms, and a great variety of pots for dried grass arrangements and plants. Some are slab built; others thrown with textured and rolled additions. She may combine these techniques and drape the piece over a hump mould whilst drying. Chris and Geoff both rub oxides of copper, manganese or iron into the textures of their pieces between biscuit firing and glazing. Chris' glaze technique is elaborate, pouring, brushing on and scraping off to achieve her effects that include blues, brownish greens and rich orange browns. The Lake District and Eden Valley have quietly influenced her work; her colours and shapes evoking the Cumbrian landscape. She sees her forms as three-dimensional paintings.

After ten years in full-time employment, Geoff decided it was time to make the break, and become a self-employed potter. So in 1989 the couple moved to Cumbria where they had previously spent many happy walking holidays. They bought land, a barn for conversion and outbuildings. Their first priority was to create a workshop from a cow byre, which they did whilst living on site in a caravan. The barn has now become their house and the outbuildings their pottery.

They work in blocks of production, alternating with periods of selling. Large craft fairs in the South are their main markets. Exhibitions in Germany and the Netherlands resulted in sales. Cumbrian outlets are Thornthwaite Gallery near Keswick, Artifacts in Arnside and Eden Craft Gallery, Penrith.

Geoff's future plans include the building of a larger, propane-fired kiln. He also aims to experiment with a glaze technique using bicarbonate of soda, that unlike salt produces no toxic fumes. Chris aims to experiment with coloured slips at the leather-hard stage. They both would like a regular exchange of ideas with other potters in the area, perhaps through the formation of a Cumbrian Potters Association.

Jon Cheney

Shop at 2 St Mary's Lane, Ambleside, Cumbria LA22 9DG   Map code S2
☎ 05394 32548

Jon is a prolific thrower and sells his work throughout Cumbria, Lancashire and Scotland. He personally delivers all his work, which keeps him in touch with his markets. His main satisfaction is knowing that his pots are for use - they are very resilient too. He is a true potter, making his living entirely from the long hours of work and dedication to his craft. Attention to finish ensures that his pots are a pleasure to feel, look at and use.

Following a year's Foundation course at Hereford, he trained for two years at Camberwell. He was extremely fortunate to be taught by Lucy Rie and the late Hans Coper. He spent the next four years in what he regards as his apprenticeship, at the Rye pottery in Sussex, where he learnt production throwing. Next he set up his own pottery in Porthleven, Cornwall, eventually employing ten staff. He sold by retail from his own premises and by wholesale throughout the area. In 1971 he moved north, briefly to Cumbria, then to the Isle of Lismore where he built his own workshop during a happy seven-year stay. He returned to Cumbria, first to Brampton and then in 1988 to Thackthwaite, where his workshop is a converted cow byre. He and his wife Heather opened a shop in Ambleside which is managed by Jane, a long-term employee of the pottery. Heather also helps with glazing and cut-out designs through leather hard lampbases, vases, aromatherapy pots and many others.

Jon unpacking his kiln at 6 o'clock one morning

The work is mainly functional domestic stoneware, made of St Thomas body with iron flecks mixed in which bleed through the glaze. This he achieves by a long soak at the end of the oxidised firing to 1280°C. His kiln is an 18 cubic foot gas-fired downdraught type. He mixes his own glazes; a white semi-matt, a *tenmoku* type, and more recently honey and blue matt glazes. Heather and Jane also make press-moulded small animals with slip and painted oxide decoration.

For relaxation he listens to music and plays the guitar. He has no plans to move again, and loves the peace and solitude of this beautiful county.

Michelle Dearden

62 Cecil Street, Carlisle, Cumbria CA1 1NX   Map code Ca2
By appointment

Michelle creates her clay musical instruments with refreshing vitality and enthusiasm, which are echoed beautifully in her colourful, vigorous and primitive designs. She extrudes a red earthenware clay to produce tubes of varying diameters, used for flutes and didjeridoos. Her ocarinas are pinch-pots. These forms are left to stiffen and then lightly burnished. Details are then carved and painted with coloured slips mixed with sand. She scratches through the slip to reveal the body clay. To give the clay maximum strength, it is fired to a relatively high temperature in an electric kiln. For her coiled drums and bongos she uses a crank mixture and wood-fires them in a raku kiln. All her pots are decorated with subjects drawn from natural history, astrology, hieroglyphics or whatever takes her fancy at the time.

Michelle's interest in ceramics began in her Foundation year at Bedford Art College, although she only spent three weeks working with clay. Her original intention was to continue with Fine Arts. However destiny brought her to Cumbria when she accepted a place on the HND course in ceramics at Cumbria College of Art and Design.

Michelle has become very happy in Cumbria, making many friends, although she had feared that ".. it was a very long way from Bedford." She completed her training in 1991 and since then she has been to many pottery and folk festivals where she has found a very positive response to her work. More locally, she has enjoyed running workshops for schoolchildren, and has more planned.

Michelle in her garden playing one of her didjeridoos

Michelle's dream is to travel round this country and abroad with a mobile pottery, making, selling and playing her instruments. She would give much pleasure to herself and others in the process. Her musical instruments add considerably to the diversity of ceramics in Cumbria.

Mike Dodd

Wellrash, Boltongate, nr Wigton, Cumbria CA5 1DH   Map code A2
☎ 09657 615
Open most of the time but confirm visit by 'phone.

Mike's pottery has its roots in Chinese and Korean traditions. Whenever possible he likes to use only authentic materials and traditional, labour-intensive methods to produce his high-fired reduction stoneware and porcelain. He loves the quality and depth of surface achieved using slips and glazes made from local materials. Cumbria is rich in minerals, and Mike takes every opportunity to use these in his work, with stunning results.

He buys clay in bulk from St Agnes in Cornwall. Whitehaven is his source of ochre used for slip. At Pass-on-Bridge, close to his home, he collects iron stone that drips out as a yellow liquid that he uses on its own as a rich over-glaze. From Shap he gets granite and hornfels, the blue-grey metamorphic stone used for road-building. Millom supplies the volcanic andesite, that is similar to hornfels and also used in his glaze compositions. For other glazes, Mike uses mixed local wood ashes although he separates some species for their particular qualities such as willow for its attractive pale green glaze that becomes greeny blue where it collects in pools. He has recently been using Corsican Pine for its lovely hues of greeny-brown, yellow and rust.

He throws on a kick-wheel making large bowls, lidded jars, bread crocks, bottles, tea-bowls, mugs and jugs, turning the bases only when necessary. His decoration methods include fluting, facetting combined with finger-combing, *scraffito* and wax-resist. Some pots are slipped then glazed followed by a second glaze. Others he double dips on the rim to give a wonderful bleed of colours that trickle down in the firing.

The 60 cu ft kiln is a down-draught design fired with wood and oil, the wood starting and finishing the process. Reduction is achieved by using a brick to restrict the oxygen intake. It may also occur naturally during the second stoking of wood. Mike feels that fly-ash enriches the glazes as it melts and etches itself into them. He glaze-fires six times a year, to between 1280°C and 1320°C. The firing cycle lasts thirteen hours.

Mike grew keen on pottery at school, through his teacher Donald Potter, but he studied medicine at Cambridge before he did a postgraduate year in ceramics at Hammersmith College of Art. He then set up his first pottery in Sussex. Many years of practical experience followed during which Mike has exhibited his work widely and also taught pottery in colleges of art. His last post was head of ceramics in Carlisle. He left in 1986 to return to full-time potting at his present premises. Mike welcomes visitors, and enjoys people taking an interest in his work. He sells about half of his work from his showroom, the remainder through exhibitions in the South.

Mike Dodd: Ash-glazed, reduced stoneware lidded jar by his garden pool

John Drinkwater

Swindale Head Farm, Bampton, Penrith, Cumbria CA10 2QT   Map code E3
☎ 0931 713323
Not open to the public

John is modest and does not enjoy publicity, disliking elitism and pretension. He believes in selling his work at prices that most people can afford. Future plans include the building of a larger up-draught kiln, fired with propane and continuing to experiment with unglazed ware and stoneware. His other interests are painting - especially landscapes, walking in the fells, local and natural history.

John trained originally in painting at Gloucester Art College, which he followed with a one-year's Postgraduate Teacher's Training course at Cardiff. During that year, he did some pottery, and the first seeds of interest were sown. He taught both History and Art for several years in South Wales, Birmingham and Horley, Surrey. In Birmingham after doing clay work with his students, he joined evening classes himself where he learned to throw and hand-build. Taking a strong liking to the latter, he gave up teaching for the next year, returned to his native Gloucestershire and bought a kiln. A part-time job in a factory provided the bare necessities, and enabled him to spend the rest of his time reading and teaching himself whilst experimenting with earthenware clay.

John found outlets for his work - mainly pinch pots, press-moulded bowls and animals - and it started selling well . He moved to Derbyshire and taught part-time, pottery-making filling the rest of his time. John found a ready market for his work, and this reinforced his decision to become a full-time potter. His last move was in 1978 to a farmhouse in a remote and beautiful valley near Haweswater, where he and his family live today. Marion, his wife, is Cumbrian.

John makes non-functional, sculptural pots, mainly woodland animals in a great variety of sizes. He avoids mass-production techniques that lead to dull standardisation. For some of his slips, he collects local clay from nearby Mardale. This he mixes with other clay, the result firing to a yellow ochre.

John digging clay in Mardale

Inset: ceramic owl

He applies texture with a variety of implements, and subsequently overlays with different slips. John mostly uses transparent glazes made from lead bisilicate, although he sometimes adds an opacifier such as zircon or rutile. For him the most important part of the firing is the long soak for up to three hours above 1000°C. This enables the iron in the body clay to act on and enrich the glazes. He sells throughout the north, supplying shops and galleries.

Edward Hughes

Isel Hall, Isel, Cockermouth, Cumbria CA13 0QG   Map code A4
☎ 0900 82557
Open by arrangement only

Edward met his Japanese wife Shizuko whilst at Bath on a degree course in ceramics. She had come to England to study English Literature. This is where their love affair with each other's country, and each other, began.

His initiation into ceramics took place at school. Edward's pottery teacher introduced him to the work of Michael Cardew, Bernard Leach and other notable potters with styles based on a blend of English slipware with oriental or African influences. Against all advice from school, he decided pottery was for him - he was hooked! Following his graduation, Edward had applied for a two-year scholarship to Kyoto University. Whilst waiting for the result he spent six months working in his former tutor's pottery studio in Crewkerne. He gained valuable experience, and also learned some of the more mundane aspects of production. In February 1977 his scholarship award arrived, and a month later he was in Kyoto. He spent the next six months having formal tuition in Japanese language. This he found it difficult to master, but persevered and grasped the rudiments, later becoming fluent.

He was then given a wheel and a corner to work in. He spent the next eighteen months learning by observation and occasional demonstrations from his master. The scholarship culminated in an exhibition of his work in the large commercial city of Osaka.

Edward and Shizuko, now married, moved into a small apartment and both found work teaching English. They were eventually able to buy materials to build a kiln and to move into premises big enough to set up their first pottery. He started making reduction fired domestic stoneware incorporating some English slipware techniques. This he sold to Japanese housewives and had his own selling exhibitions each year.

After five years of potting in Japan Edward felt nostalgic for the English tradition, with which he feared he was losing touch. The couple returned to England in 1984 and bought a cottage at Renwick where he set up his second pottery. Five years on and Edward needed more space. By a curious and timely coincidence he met Mary Burkett, former director of the Abbot Hall Museum in Kendal. She offered him the use of part of the buildings at Isel Hall to live and work in. He accepted and following some restoration work, he built his present 70 cu ft propane fired down-draught kiln.

Edward at home in Isel with Tenmoku glazed teapot and cups

William Plumptre: Stoneware pots with roped decoration, slip inlay and Japanese brushwork.

Edward Hughes: Large stoneware platter with slip-combed decoration.

Edward now throws beautiful fluted bowls, large plates with deep foot rings and other decorative and domestic ware. He makes tiles and also slab-builds lidded boxes and shallow-sided rectangular trays. His body clay is a white St Thomas stoneware that he wedges with iron oxide, staining it a warm brown. His slips are mainly dark iron or white and may be trailed, feathered or combed onto a slip ground. The pots are glazed with *tenmoku*, *celadon*, or *chun* and reduction fired to about 1300°C.

Although Edward works in a meticulous and organised way, paying great attention to detail and finish, his pots have a spontaneity and freedom of form and decoration that is quite breathtaking. He sells most of his work through exhibitions in Japan. Each year he ships out a container, with up to four hundred pieces. Otherwise he sells through Galerie Besson in London and from his premises. He strongly believes in pricing his work at the proper market value and rightly does not undersell himself.

William Plumptre

Fell Yeat, Hartsop, Patterdale, Penrith, Cumbria CA11 0NZ Map code E9
☎ 07684 82545
Open 10 am to 6 pm by appointment

William lives with his wife and son in the hamlet of Hartsop, between Brothers Water and Kirkstone Pass. He is surrounded by beautiful soaring fells that are also home to red deer. His farmhouse home is stone-built under a green slate roof in the traditional style. The similar outbuildings are now used for his pottery. When time allow, he enjoys fishing, walking his three lurcher dogs and motorbike racing.

William was born and raised in the south, but spent many happy family holidays in this area. When the opportunity arose, it seemed a natural place to live and work. William went to school in Dorset where he was taught by the potter Ian Gregory. He found himself drawn to the work of oriental potters. In 1983, William completed a three-year ceramic design course at Chelsea College of Art. He then spent the next two years painting pictures whilst contemplating his future direction. Takeshi Yasuda, a Japanese potter friend, persuaded William to continue his pottery studies in Japan. William already had this idea in mind, but just needed a final push. Armed only with a list of contacts, William arrived in Mashiko in 1985, and almost immediately found work. He spent the next six months throwing tea-cups before moving on for a similar period with a kiln-builder. The following year he spent working for the master potter Tatsuzo Shimaoka. Once more he was given a wheel and clay and once more the task of throwing the same simple shape. The training regime was rigorous; six weeks throwing, then packing and unpacking kilns, glazing and decorating. As their part in the glazing process, apprentices were only allowed to sponge excess glaze from the bottoms of the pots. In 1987 William returned to England and Hartsop to set up his own first pottery and built an oil-fired 35 cu ft down-draught kiln.

William makes outstanding decorative stoneware, including tea-pots often faceted with iron oxide brushwork, and large plates, bowls, bottles and vases. He impresses texture with rope, inlays cobalt and copper slips and uses other techniques such as fluting, combing, *scraffito* and brushwork. He mixes his own wood ash and *tenmoku* glazes. He is currently experimenting with Kirkstone green slate as a glaze ingredient. He glaze-fires to about 1280°C under a reducing atmosphere for the latter part of the firing. William sells his work through exhibitions in London and Edinburgh, through the Castlegate House Gallery in Cockermouth and twice a year from his own premises.

Lorna Graves

Apple Tree House, Hunsonby, Penrith, Cumbria CA10 1PN   Map code E5
☎ 0768 881710
Visits by appointment only

Lorna considers herself as a painter and ceramic sculptor, devoting an equal amount of time to both. Some of her sculptures are cast in bronze at a foundry. Her drawings are complete in themselves, but Lorna finds they subconsciously surface through her clay sculpture after some time has elapsed. Lorna is a Cumbrian, who spent ten years of her life in the south but has lived here for the remainder. She draws her inspiration from the land, fells and skies of the Eden valley. Her paintings have movement but the sculptures have a stillness. She finds it a challenge to try and reconcile these conflicts.

Lorna hand-builds, using raku clay. She makes the basic shape of her components. The larger ones are hollowed out, and then she joins the parts together and refines the exterior shape by paring down with a knife. Lorna uses a serrated tool to create texture, and when the form is dry, she may use sandpaper to finish. If she wants a bone-like surface, she taps it gently against a smooth wooden board.

Raku animal form

Lorna enjoying the atmosphere at the Long Meg Stone Circle near Hunsonby

Her source material originally came from a dream she had twenty-five years ago. It was about an animal form that seemed vulnerable and was in the middle of a city. She made a naïve pastel drawing of it and eventually produced its image in clay. This animal form, for which Lorna is well-known, has many mutations. She continues making them in response to requests. She feels that she has subconsciously followed this animal ever since. It has evolved with a rider, human figures lying on its back, or on their sides, and more recently, a bird, moon or wing. Boats with figures lying down in them now have wings as sails. Lorna interprets the human body as the consciousness; the wing is the link between earth, body, spirit and sky. She makes mystic temples and shrines some with hidden secrets, and celestial subjects.

Following a low biscuit firing, Lorna paints on copper oxide, with an alkaline frit. Some areas of the piece are painted more thickly than others. She sometimes rubs oxide into the texture and then washes it off, leaving only slight traces. She enjoys the quality obtained by this combined with the raku secondary firing. The pieces are individually removed with tongs, and placed in wood shavings, hay or leaves. Following this, the small sculptures are placed in water to arrest the firing.

Lorna had always felt that she was an artist but had initially followed an academic path, studying geography and geology at university in London, then calligraphy at Cambridge. As her calligraphy began to turn into art she realised her interest lay in marks and shapes. At that point she knew she had the courage to become an artist. Lorna came back to her roots in Cumbria and studied Fine Art for three years at Cumbria College of Art and Design. Geoff Barnfather, head of Fine Art, introduced her to clay and raku firing. She was very taken with the results and has not looked back. She now makes what she feels "as it comes pouring out of her". Lorna has exhibited in Britain, America and Japan. Her work is in many public collections. She sells through galleries in London and Edinburgh, the Isis Gallery, Melmerby and from her studio.

The Wetheriggs Pottery

Clifton Dykes, Penrith, Cumbria CA10 2DH   Map code E11
☎0768 62946
Open daily 10 to 6

The beehive kiln now houses examples of early Wetheriggs wares

Wetheriggs is one of the few remaining English country potteries to have survived the ravages of wars, social change and changes of fashion. The bee-hive kiln is the only remaining example of the type. It now forms part of the museum that is being established by Peter Strong. He has a marvellous collection of old slip-ware from all parts of the country which will eventually be displayed in the museum.

Peter Strong acquired the site in 1990, and is bringing back to Wetheriggs large-scale production, once thought to have been relegated to history. The previous owners, Jonathan and Dorothy Snell had done a lot of restoration and renovation during the preceding twenty years. Peter is continuing this work, and the pottery is going from strength to strength, with the help of his two throwers, Russell and Alastair. David Drewery has recently joined the team, and is establishing the mould-making and slip-casting department.

The range of glazed slipware being produced has the traditional slip-trailed designs used by the Schofields, the first potters on the site. For coloured slips and glazes they use blues, greens, browns, honey yellows and creamy whites.

They continue making salt-kits, the speciality of Wetheriggs, kitchen ware and the more ornamental cradles, bird money-boxes, frog mugs, puzzle jugs and loving cups.

There is an extensive variety of terra cotta garden ware, including strawberry pots, long toms, Edwardian seed trays, bonsai pots, ornate urns, Victorian jardinieres and path edgings. To complement these, they opened a garden centre in 1992.

A selection of typical Wetheriggs slip-trailed wares in the showroom

Peter Strong

Peter is very much an exponent and disciple of the English slip-ware tradition, and is a purist in the sense that he does not feel the need for his pots to be influenced by oriental or African wares of the Leach and Cardew styles. Peter studied ceramics on a Foundation course and subsequently Fine Art and sculpture in his native Essex. For the next four years he worked at a pottery in Colchester, and occasionally for a commercial sculptor. After a short period of unemployment he became ceramics technician at Mid-Essex Technical College, where Joanna Constantinidis was the head of the School of Art. She sometimes allowed him to deputise for her teaching evening classes. With her encouragement, Peter was accepted for a BA in ceramics at Camberwell where one of his contemporaries was Jim Malone. During his first year at Camberwell he worked with Peter Dick at Coxwold, Yorkshire where he was introduced to George Curtis who made large gardenware pots from his own seam of clay at nearby Ripon. Peter frequently returned to visit Dick and Curtis, because he was drawn to their pottery.

In 1975 Peter set up for himself on the site of the run-down Soil Hill pottery, formerly run by Isaac Button. He sold his wares on a market stall and in a shop in Halifax. In 1979 he moved to Clapham in Yorkshire, establishing a second pottery, and spent the next ten years mainly making gardenware. He continued to supply outlets that he had gained whilst in Halifax. He became good friends with Peter Brears, the authority on English country pottery. Wetheriggs was put up for sale in 1989. Peter badly needed more space. This was his dream, a unique opportunity that he could not miss.

David Drewery

Peter Strong recently found some old plaster moulds and press-moulds which David is now restoring and re-modelling, and adapting them for use with casting slip. The clay he uses for casting comes direct from the quarry and is processed at the pottery. It is first mixed with water in a large blunger, screened and then pumped through into a smaller blunger in the mould-making room.

David is currently modelling and sculpting a series of wall planters based on elaborate Victorian designs from which he will make moulds. He is working on a range of bonsai pots to be open-cast, and is already casting lion's feet for large urns.

He has qualifications in art and design and a diploma in ceramics as well as an honours degree in Industrial Design. His past experience includes establishing a pottery and a porcelain factory in Scotland. David also worked as a freelance designer for several ceramics factories in Stoke-on-Trent. He is a highly skilled technician and talented ceramic artist who is bound to make his mark on Wetheriggs.

David sculpting the original for a mould

Russell Gibbs

Russell believes that to become a good thrower with a sense of form, needs lots of practice. Those intending to learn should not be too precious about what they make but must be objective and critical. He believes that quantity is the benchmark, and with luck, in time quality will follow. Russell loves to experiment with glazes and shapes in his free time, and has become a dedicated, enthusiastic and talented potter.

Russell studied ceramics on a two-year HND course at Cumbria College of Art and Design, and met Peter when he came to give a demonstration. He later went to Peter's Clapham Pottery to gain work experience. In 1988 Russell again went to work with Peter in Clapham, whilst doing a further year of study at Rochdale. When in 1990, Peter moved to Wetheriggs Russell came with him, and he is now responsible for throwing the garden ware. Now Peter and Russell have adapted the large gas kiln, that had two chambers into a one-chamber, split-draught kiln and enabling them to widen their range of large gardenware.

Alistair Wills

Alistair started working here as an assistant during Jonathan Snell's last year. When Peter took over, he offered Alistair the opportunity of staying on. Alistair grew up in Appleby, and when he left school, he was unsure what he wanted to do. When he first started at Wetheriggs, to him it was just a job. After five years, it has become very much more, and now Alistair enjoys his work as a potter. He has become very proficient at slip-trailing, using the traditional cow-horn and goose quill, becoming an important member of the team.

Victoria and Michael Eden

Parkside, Hale, Milnthorpe, Cumbria LA7 7BL   Map code S4
☎ 05395 62342
Open by arrangement

Victoria first trained as a teacher, and then spent two years in Thailand working for Voluntary Service Overseas. On her return in 1976 she got a Diploma in Ceramics after two years study at Lancaster. She set up her first pottery at Wolf House Gallery, Silverdale, where she made slip-decorated red earthenware. Stoneware in the Leach tradition was the vogue at the time, but Victoria followed her own instincts and enjoyed the wider range of colours available at earthenware temperatures.

Michael was working in forestry and nature conservation when they met in 1980 although he had a background in print-making and art. In 1981 shortly after their marriage , Michael began studying pottery at night classes, and his natural abilities soon surfaced. They bought a shop, Multum-in-Parvo, in Kendal where they made and sold their work. For the first three years Michael worked part-time in landscape architecture before going to full-time pottery in 1984.

Slip-trailed and scraffito decorated earthenware plate

They moved to the present address in 1987 - an idyllic setting for their young family - and converted outbuildings for their workshop. Michael keeps sheep and maintains grassland to encourage wild flowers. Victoria is happy bringing up their two children, and pots for a lesser part of the time. She expects to resume full-time potting when the children are older.

The Edens have developed a range of standard lines which they sell wholesale all over the country. Most pots are thrown, but they have designed some moulds for slip-casting and press-moulding. This aids the production of more decorative pieces, such as their vases, jugs, candelabra and "fish" tea-pots, which are part of the extensive range. The pots are decorated with many colours of slip, sometimes trailed or sponge-stencilled onto a slip ground. Impressed leaves are stamped, or scratched-through *scraffito* designs may be added. Michael avoids turning where possible. He creates a fluted foot by using a rib with a profile cut-out. The pots are raw-glazed and fired up to 1115°C in an electric kiln. They mix their own clear glaze of lead bisilicate, china clay and bentonite.Their work has movement, a wealth of colour, and a very tactile quality.

They teach at night classes and run pottery holidays in the summer. They have built two kilns, one for Raku, the other to fire with wood, using both for teaching purposes and to enable them to experiment.

Gordon Fox

Kentmere Pottery, Kentmere, Nr Kendal, Cumbria LA8 9JH   Map code S5
☎ 0539 821621
Open all year but best to telephone

Gordon lives and works in an idyllic situation in the Kentmere valley. The beauty and tranquillity around him seem to be reflected in the richness and elegance of his pottery. After many years' experience, Gordon has reached the stage where he can sell all his work from his well-appointed showroom on the premises. He has built up a following both national and international and posts orders all over the world.

His work is highly refined earthenware. Although functional, it is very decorative, employing motifs such as flowers, trees and animals. His range includes lampbases with turned wooden bases, pot pourri and nut bowls, vases, candlesticks, napkin rings and jardinieres. He takes commissions for pieces that complement clients' fabrics and wallpapers used in design schemes for lounges and bedrooms.

Gordon throws pots on the wheel, and when leather-hard, he turns the bases to refine them. Other methods he employs are slipcasting and using a jig and jolley. A light burnishing follows for the finish. Brushwork is one of his favourite activities and he spends hours perfecting butterflies. He stamps and impresses leaves, flowers or seed heads, attaches sprigs and may add exquisite little garlands of porcelain flowers. Using underglaze or onglaze he then subtly colours them. To enhance or emphasise his forms, he paints on enamels and gold lustre that are fired on during a third, low-temperature firing.

From their home in Lancaster, Gordon's family often holidayed in the Lake District. When seventeen and on a visit to Ambleside, he happened to visit George F Cook's pottery. George was one of the new breed of Art College trained potters, who made stoneware. Gordon was enthralled by the rapid transformation of lumps of clay on the wheel, and became determined to learn for himself. He wrote to George offering to work for nothing, being prepared to do anything, however menial. George was taken by this offer, and agreed to it although he did not normally employ untrained staff. Over the next seven years Gordon served his apprenticeship, experiencing all parts of the production process, learning by observation and at first hand. When he was ready to set up his own pottery, he decided to make fine earthenware that enabled him to use a wide range of colours. Gordon's current prices are commensurate with the many processes and stages required to achieve the very high standards he sets himself.

Gordon Fox: Small earthenware jug with fine snowdrop brushwork, impressed decoration and embellished with gold lustre

Bob Entwistle

Hard Ing, Sleagill, near Morland, Penrith CA10 3HD   Map code E4
☎ 0931 714404
Open to public by arrangement

Bob's main purpose in potting is to produce functional pots, which also have aesthetic value. His other interests include vernacular architecture, industrial archaeology and sculpture in the environment. Future plans include experimenting with slip-decorated stoneware, and building a propane-fired kiln.

After his training at Manchester Art College, Bob worked at the Briglin Pottery in London. He returned to Manchester and lectured in Ceramics for three years.

Bob's muscular arms are typical of a potter

The middle year of the three was spent at Charlotte Mason College in Ambleside. That spell in Ambleside made him decide to live in Cumbria and his next home for a year was the Wetheriggs Pottery near Penrith where he gained further experience in making traditional slip-decorated earthenware and terra cotta gardenware. Bob then married Lynne and moved to Shap where he set up his first pottery and shop, producing mainly slip-ware and some porcelain. After six years he outgrew the premises and decided to move to a cottage at Sleagill, overlooking the Eden valley, where he has much more space and seclusion. The cottage was restored and the outbuildings converted into his present workshop. This enabled him to increase the extent and variety of pots to include large gardenware. He now sells throughout the North in galleries, craft shops and garden centres.

Slip-trailed earthenware teapot and mug

Bob is very much a man of the people, gregarious and a natural communicator. Eager to share his vision and skills, he has a strong commitment to three-dimensional art in education, and teaches part-time, also running workshops for both children and adults in the community.

Hans Ulrich

Turning Point, 117 Highgate, Kendal, Cumbria LA9 4EN   Map code S12
☎ 0539 732734
Open normal shop hours.

Hans has evolved his slipware from the English traditional style, making two different types of domestic and decorative earthenware pottery. One is made from a buff clay, onto which blue slip designs are trailed on when leather hard. After the biscuit firing these pots are given a white semi-opaque tin glaze. He uses red earthenware for the other more complex type, and these are dipped in white slip when leather hard. Red clay slip is next used to create trailed outlines of a design which often feature farmyard animals or celestial subjects. Following a biscuit firing, glaze is trailed into some of the outlined areas. The pots are given a second biscuit firing, which has the effect of crazing the glazed regions. He then trails on more glaze, some honey coloured, some stained blue with cobalt, which is allowed to seep into the crazes. The third firing to glaze temperature merges the crazes, which disappear. The final brilliant colours are a unique combination of apparently effortless painting and triple firing.

Hans was born in Carlisle and grew up in Cockermouth. After the Art Foundation Course in Carlisle, he studied painting and sculpture for three years in Hull. He next spent a year at the Findhorn community where he made stoneware pottery. Whilst there he met Jonathon Snell who shortly afterwards was to take over the run-down Wetheriggs Pottery. Hans returned to Cumbria to join the Snells in their six month period on trial. He stayed there altogether two years, potting and helping with restoration.

In 1973 Hans decided to set up his own pottery and shop in Cleator Moor. After three years he moved to Whitehaven, where he supplied wholesalers and sold from his shop, at craft fairs and agricultural shows. When his lease expired in 1986 he bought his present premises in Kendal, using the basement for his pottery and selling his wares in the shop above. He has gradually introduced other complementary items for sale in the shop. Hans' pots are also on sale at The Village Bakery in Melmerby.

Hans has since moved his home nearby to rural Skelsmergh where he keeps ducks, geese and hens, practices organic gardening and spends as much time as possible with his young family. He is in the process of installing his pottery into the outbuildings.

Facing page:
Karen Woof: Coiled, burnished and smoke-fired earthenware pot
Hans Ulrich: Slipware cockerel platter at Red Bank Farm, Skelsmergh

Hans Ulrich: Slipware cockerel platter at Red Bank Farm.

Karen Woof: Coiled, burnished and smoke-fired pot.

Karen Woof

c/o Victoria and Michael Eden, Parkside, Hale, Milnthorpe, Cumbria LA7 7BL   Map code S13
☎ 05395 63342
Open by arrangement

Most of Karen's work is hand-built - she finds coiling very therapeutic. Her pots are personal derivations of the African tradition. The forms are often large-scale, spherical and curvaceous with rounded rims. She uses a red earthenware body and sometimes brushes on a fine red clay slip (*terra sigilatta*), an ideal ground for burnishing. When the pots are leather-hard she begins burnishing with a silver spoon, using a circular motion. This has the effect of consolidating the larger particles which are pushed into the clay and the finer particles come to the surface. She repeats the process and the resulting sheen gives the pots a luscious appearance. Some *scraffito* scratched patterns are added before a slow even drying, after which the pots are fired to 950°C in an electric kiln. Some are finished inside with a low temperature lead bisilicate glaze in this same firing. The second firing is in pine sawdust, which burns and smoulders for about thirty-six hours. Small pots are layered between sawdust and newspaper in an oil drum. Larger pieces are fired in a pit. Ashes and broken pots are distributed between the wares in order deliberately to expose or avoid blackened areas.

Karen also makes some glazed and functional ware - coiled bowls and slip-cast lamp bases, which she coats with a white clay slip. When they are bone dry she paints on under-glaze colours and wax-resists some areas. She scratches designs through the slip and paints cobalt into these lines. They are glaze fired to 1110°C using a transparent glaze.

Karen's interest in pottery began through helping Victoria Eden. She took a Foundation Course at Preston followed by a BA in ceramics at Bath Academy of Art. After training, she worked for a short while with Victoria in Kendal before spending a year with a graphic designer, where Karen had her own studio. Two more years were spent making slip-cast lamp bases for another potter before Karen moved to Milnthorpe in 1989. By this time Victoria and Michael Eden had married and moved from Kendal, and Karen has shared their workshop ever since. She sells her work through galleries and exhibitions in Cumbria and further afield. She teaches part-time at three local colleges and also finds time to enjoy the outdoor activities that attract so many people to this area.

Patiently burnishing her coiled pot. The image of Karen hand-building was the inspiration for the trailed design on the plate commissioned for the book's front cover.

Meryll Evans

Nandi Hills, Lonsties, Keswick, Cumbria CA12 4TD   Map code A3
☎ 07687 73057
Visit only by appointment

Meryll's home has magnificent views overlooking Derwentwater and the surrounding fells. She is a portrait painter and sculptor who has established a reputation by the sensitive and perceptive way she interprets her subjects. She works almost exclusively to commission, for exhibitions and private collections. The majority of her work is sculpted in red earthenware clay, the remainder cast at a foundry. She may use clay, wax or plaster to sculpt the original forms for casting. These are usually for limited editions and are produced in resin-bronze, bronze or plaster. Her clay busts are modelled solid, halved, hollowed out then re-joined. On request, she will patinate the terra cotta.

Meryll trained in art, first at Cheltenham then Birmingham. Next she taught art in a Reading school and joined the university's extra-mural department to study Fine Art. After two years, she married and went to live in Kenya where her husband was stationed in the army. They remained there after the war when her husband obtained a post at Jeanes School, a training centre established for ex-servicemen. Meryll began painting portraits, for friends at first but gradually she gained commissions for children's portraits. She met a German sculptor, Karl Michels, who invited her to sculpt in his studio. As soon as she got her hands in the local red clay she felt this was for her. Later, when Karl went to America she continued sculpting and managed to get a firing at a local tile factory. The Kenya Art and Craft Society exhibited her work. She thoroughly enjoyed designing scenery sets for The National Theatre in Nairobi.

In 1965 Meryll and Archie returned to Keswick. Meryll became Head of Art at Keswick School where she found an unused wheel and kiln. She decided to study at Cumbria College of Art and Design, learning to throw, mix glazes and fire a kiln so as to give the children fuller use of the school's resources.

Eight years on and Meryll left teaching, but continued her contact with the Cumbria College. She started making tea-pots in stoneware and porcelain, established her own workshop at home and became a member of the Guild of Lakeland Craftsmen. In spite of finding markets for her work, she was not entirely happy and thankfully returned to her red clay. Meryll gradually began receiving commissions for terra cotta sculptures, working to her own photographs or drawings of her subjects. Commissions were also forthcoming for reliefs of artists and poets. In 1983, she submitted several pieces to the prestigious Lake Art Society. Acceptance marked a turning point in her development as an artist.

Relief sculpture

Stemming from her many years in Kenya, Meryll has made a series of statuettes and heads of African women and children. She has had work commissioned by the WRAC for presentation to the Queen Mother and the Duchess of Kent. As a result of these, a commission followed from the Royal Transport Corps in Germany.

Mike Labrum

Spiral Pottery, Zeffirelli's Arcade, Ambleside, Cumbria LA22 9AD   Map code S8
☎ 05394 46967 or 05394 33845
Pottery and shop open Monday to Saturday, 10 am to 5 pm.

Mike came to Penrith to teach Art and General Subjects at a boys' primary school. He had always wanted to be a painter, and after leaving school he trained at Streatham College of Education in General Art and Ceramics. Even though he grew up in the south, he felt surprisingly at home in Cumbria. He later found out that one of his grandmothers had lived in Carlisle. Whilst exploring the Penrith area, he discovered Wetheriggs Pottery, and became a friend of the Snells and a regular visitor. One summer holiday they asked if he would like to help there, and he stayed for the next three years. He learned all the aspects of making earthenware pottery as well as whatever else needed doing. Mike eventually decided that he wanted to learn about other types of pottery, and enrolled in the HND course at Cumbria College of Art & Design in Carlisle. He found that the time he had spent at Wetheriggs had been invaluable, enabling him to concentrate there on other aspects of pot-making, and to experiment with decoration and glaze techniques. Mike felt that studying ceramics as a mature student had worked very well for him, and had enabled him to see clearly where his interests lay. He teaches meditation and Yoga in his spare time. For relaxation he also enjoys drawing and painting landscapes, fell-walking and photography.

He returned to Wetheriggs when he had completed his training. Meanwhile the Snells had decided to branch out and open a pottery studio and shop in Ambleside. They found suitable premises at the Zeffirelli complex, and installed Mike there. He threw and decorated wares on the premises, and took them to Wetheriggs to be glazed and fired. After a year it became clear that the arrangements were not financially viable, and the Snells decided to pull out. Mike however chose to stay, and set up on his own in 1984 when he bought an electric wheel and kiln and began making oxidised stoneware.

His products now include tea-pots, coffee sets, vases, jugs and numerous other small items. Mike has developed a wide range of glazes and decoration techniques. He has perfected a slip-glaze that he trails on to biscuit ware. In his most recent designs, Mike has used a combination of painted slip and wax-resist, which he then enhances with his glazes. These glazes include a *tenmoku* type, a copper-green transparent one that he pours and overlaps to produce pleasing effects, and two whites - one zinc-based, the other a dolomite matt. He now sells a wide variety of original work.

Mike welcomes visitors to his workshop in the lively Zeffirelli Arcade

Tobias Harrison

Swallow Barn, High Newton, Nr Grange-over-Sands, Cumbria LA11 6NZ   Map code S6
☎ 05395 31231
Open by appointment only

Tobias's pots positively gleam with opulence. Their beauty is quite undeniable. The forms are refined with precision and enhanced by the depth of colour and lustre applied. Elaborate and ornate handles seem to grow from the pots that they embellish. He makes special commissions, often commemorative, which may feature elegant gold calligraphy that he paints freehand.

Tobias grew up in Windermere. His introduction to ceramics began at school in Yorkshire and he became specially interested in the work of Chinese potters. After he left school he spent two years at Lancaster Art College, moving to the Central School of Art, where he took a degree in ceramics. For the next three years he worked at the Chelsea Pottery as a thrower.

He set up his first pottery at Grasmere, renting a National Trust house. He had by now set his mind on making lustre ware, enjoying the various effects that were possible. Tobias continued making some items for the Chelsea Pottery, which he sent to them by post. Eventually he moved his studio to a barn in High Newton, where his artist parents live nearby.

At first he used white earthenware and porcelain, but now uses a white-firing North Devon ball clay prepared for him at Stoke-on-Trent. Tobias deliberately throws all his pots quite heavily. The major part of the work begins at the leather-hard stage. He turns his pots on a chuck to create the final smooth and well-defined forms. He completes the process by burnishing with a flexible kidney and a spoon. He fires in an electric kiln; the biscuit firing is high, to 1100°C; a low glaze to 1060°C; and the third, lustre firing to 710°C.

For larger ware he mixes grog into the body clay in his enormous de-airing pug-mill. The glazes and lustres are sprayed and brushed or air-brushed on. For his greens he uses a chrome glaze into which he mixes cobalt grains, as copper does not work well with lustre. Pinks are produced by a tin-vanadium mix that gives some opacity and, with lustre-added, iridescence too.

He also makes complex ceramic electric fires and lamps with intricate cut-out designs. The larger versions are thrown in sections, joined and turned. For this work he uses a wide range of coloured glazes and lustres, including platinum and gold. The forms are evocative of China.

Several galleries in Cumbria and beyond sell his work, which is also available from his own premises. He owns a collection of motorbikes, and enjoys racing, trials and hill-climb sprinting; an unusual and incongruous combination.

Tobias painting lustre onto one of his bowls

Liz Lark

Artist in Residence, Casterton School, Kirkby Lonsdale, Cumbria LA6 2SG   Map code S9
By arrangement only

Liz is an artist in the widest sense. Her work revolves around themes of the human form. Colour, texture, movement and music are important aspects of her completed works. She uses clay as her main means of expression in three dimensions. As a basis on which to begin and as an extension of the life form, Liz chose the shape of the cello. She also sculpts treasure chests, drawing inspiration from mediæval French originals. Her surface textures and colours are reminiscent of crumbling buildings with bleached or peeling paint.

She has constructed plaster moulds to form the basic shapes, and made press moulds for the appendages. She begins by randomly brushing different coloured slips into the mould. The spaces in-between she fills with a neutral-coloured slip. Her clay, a multi-purpose crank, is then pressed into the mould. To complete the box-like shape, a lid is similarly formed, and when both are stiffened they are joined together. The whole piece is then removed from the mould and undergoes modification whilst resting on a thick layer of foam. It is cut and manipulated, when any cracks are exaggerated and extended before sprigs are added. She may then apply more slips and oxides. After drying, the pieces are biscuit-fired.

Liz has two different methods of glaze firing. She raku fires in an oil drum lined with fire bricks and fuelled with propane gas. A low temperature glaze is applied to the pieces which she then places, using tongs, in the pre-heated kiln. Larger heavy pieces are first put in the kiln and brought up to temperature. On removal, the sculptures are quenched in sawdust, resulting in smoky blacks and metallic copper sheens. For her second method, she applies matt stoneware glazes saturated with oxides and body stains. She deliberately under-fires these to 1100°C in her electric kiln, to achieve her desired matt and chalky finish.

Stoneware cello form

Liz's formal art training began with a Foundation course at Bath. She spent the next year looking after adults with learning difficulties. After three years in Cardiff, she obtained a BA in ceramics. Since then she has taught ceramics at Casterton School. During the summer, she takes ceramics workshop at The Practice Place, a health-orientated holiday centre in Crete. She has held many exhibitions which have formed the basis of her sales, although she enjoys undertaking commissions.

Peter Lascelles

Pennine Pottery, Clargill Head House, Alston, Cumbria CA9 3NG   Map code E6
☎ 0434 381257
Open daily, except Mondays

For many years Peter was a biology teacher at St Paul's School in London. He has always been a keen collector of pottery, with Michael Casson, David Leach and John Maltby among his favourites. In 1982 he started attending pottery evening classes given by the art teacher at St Paul's and after two years of this study, he continued potting in his spare time. The opportunity of early retirement from teaching allowed him to channel his increasing enthusiasm for clay into starting a new career as a potter. The family decided to look for a suitable property in which to set up a pottery, shop and café, and whilst on holiday, chanced across the tea-room at Clargill Head House. On chatting with the owner they discovered that the property was soon to be put up for sale, so details were discussed and a price agreed there and then. In July 1992 they moved to their new house high up in the remote and beautiful North Pennines. They have converted the outbuildings to a pottery and their shop and café, which serves delicious home-baked food, opened at Easter 1993.

Peter uses both red earthenware and a stoneware St Thomas' body for his garden ware. He enjoys throwing large pots and has an adapted raised wheel-head enabling him to work freely and unrestricted by the wheel tray. He uses stoneware clay for all his glazed ware. Peter gains pleasure from making kitchen ware and describes his work as both functional and decorative. One of his hobbies is cooking, and this helps him with his designs. His knowledge and love of plants helps in the same way with his planters and garden pots. Peter also takes commissions for commemorative plates and personalised items.

Peter's other preoccupation - his pipe

His stoneware is decorated with oxide-stained slip made from equal parts of ball clay and china clay. To some pots he adds decorative handles and lugs. On others he applies bands and geometric designs of slip, sometimes including wax- or paper-resist techniques. He mixes his own glazes, which are normally transparent. Using propane, he fires to 1260°C in an oxidising atmosphere.

Jim Malone

Hagget House, Towngate, Ainstable, Carlisle, Cumbria CA4 9RE   Map code E7
☎ 076886 444
Shop and pottery open 8am to 8pm all year round.

Jim is the true essence of an artist-potter. He makes no compromise to quality nor fashion. There are no short cuts to producing pottery of this superb quality. Local materials predominate; ochre from Alston for slip, wood ash from beech and silver birch, and granite from Shap for glazes. His every process is labour intensive, such as his firings, which take up to 24 hours continuous stoking. Wood off-cuts from a local saw-mill are burnt to achieve 400°C, then oil to 1000°C, and the final surge to 1300°C is attained with wood. Reduction is achieved by reducing the air intake and more stoking. Fly ash settles on the pots and volatilises, adding more character to the final glazes.

He built his own two-chamber climbing kiln, which has a cross-draught design. Jim's wife and family all assist with the firings, which take place about every three months. His kick-wheel is of a Korean design with no tray and a small wheel head which he has adapted to accommodate tall pots. Of necessity he uses fairly soft clay and very little water. The rhythm of throwing on a kick-wheel is consistent with his adherence to authentic methods. The clay bodies are mainly a standard ball-clay and fire-clay mixture, and also a dark, high iron-bearing body for use with the decorative technique, *Hakeme* (a thin slip is brushed on in broad strokes, leaving some brush texture and the iron to burn through). He also uses some semi-porcelainous stoneware for tea bowls. Other techniques for decoration that he uses include impressed pads of clay, incising, combing and fine brush decoration with oxides often combined with the use of slips. His products are bottles, jugs bowls and other domestic ware.

Jim was originally a teacher of English and Art, but inspired by a visit to the Victoria and Albert Museum, he decided on a change of career. Ian Godfrey and Colin Pearson were major influences during his pottery studies at Camberwell. A move to the Winchcombe Pottery in Gloucestershire enabled him to study further with Ray Finch. Jim set up his own first pottery in Wales and began producing high-fired stoneware. Gradually his sales increased and his reputation grew. He has exhibited both here and abroad, and museums, including the Victoria and Albert Museum own examples of his work. In 1983, Jim moved to Cumbria and spent the next few years at the Cumbria College of Art and Design, teaching with Mike Dodd. Both Jim and Mike have now returned to full-time pottery. Jim's work is found in a large number of selective outlets, including his own premises.

Jim Malone: Reduced stoneware jug, with combed and stamped decoration in relief, photographed on the step of his workshop

Adrian Newnham

Sunyn Cottage, Soutergate, Kirkby-in-Furness, Cumbria LA17 7TW   Map code S10
☎ 0229 89517
Can be visited by arrangement

Adrian loves natural history and the environment. Elements of these come through in his pottery, especially his tree and fungi forms that he hand builds. He rolls out slabs of clay on newspaper, then impresses bark texture. He wraps and folds the clay round a cylinder for support until it has stiffened, when the cylinder is removed and a clay base added. He attaches modelled roots, lichens and fungi formed by rolling and pinching the clay. He uses a crank mixture for the main trunk and white earthenware for the additions.

Other wares are functional but decorative, comprising bowl forms, planters, vases, candle-holders, and pot pourri pots of varying sizes. Adrian is experimenting with casting ceramic eggs and then suspending them on refractory wire in the glaze firing.

The other pots are white earthenware that are slip-cast in open moulds that he makes himself. He enjoys the reliability of casting the basic form that he then modifies by crimping, carving or piercing tree designs round the rim. He biscuit fires and then waxes the bases. Next he glazes with zircon white or a pink commercial stained glaze. This is followed by splashing on copper or cobalt oxide which gives combinations of blues, greens, pinks and creamy whites. The pots are glaze fired in an electric kiln to between 1100°C and 1150°C. Pots with copper in their glaze are fired together (to prevent other wares becoming contaminated as copper floats in the kiln atmosphere). He sells his work through craft galleries, craft fairs and from his premises as well as taking special commissions.

Adrian grew up in Oxfordshire, before training as a Secondary School teacher at Charlotte Mason College in Ambleside. He specialised in Art and Environmental Studies, and meanwhile developed a love for Cumbria that made him not want to leave. He taught at Coniston, Kendal and Barrow before his present post at Dalton Junior School. The children there enjoy clay work so much that they call to see him in his studio and "help".

His interest in ceramics surfaced gradually, but has now become a very important part of his life. Adrian is a very cheerful. energetic and lively person who thoroughly enjoys both teaching and potting. He also manages to find time to organise a local football team, and goes walking and fishing too after he has finished work on the extensions to his house.

Bob March

Hutton Lodge, Soulby, Kirkby Stephen, Cumbria CA17 4PL   Map code E8
☎ 07683 71396
Can be visited by arrangement

Bob's career has been exciting and varied, with pottery featuring since 1975. He trained with Giles Parrott, and subsequently managed to combine pottery with an army career, culminating in the establishment of a craft centre in Oman. After five successful years there, he returned to England and taught pottery part-time at Preston and York. This was followed by his setting up a small pottery in the army school at Strensall near York, which he ran for eighteen months.

Bob and his wife now live in a splendid old sandstone house in the upper Eden valley. Scandal Beck winds through their large garden and the woodlands beyond. Their geese enjoy the freedom to wander at will. The rural setting seems timeless and a million miles away from Bob's life in the British Army. He was still enlisted in 1986 when he set up the pottery at Soulby, and he spent a further five years in the army whilst working part-time making pottery, mainly to commission.

He uses a white semi-porcelain body for his finely thrown domestic ware and he also makes large terra cotta gardenware. Bob decorates his pots when bone-dry but unfired, using oxide-stained slips made from the body clay and underglaze colours. He then brushes on delicate decoration and finally adds a transparent glaze that results in blues and browns on a white background. His pots are fired to 1260°C in an electric kiln. At present he is working on glaze recipes using local stone from the Hartley Quarry.

Bob now pots full-time, and having outgrown his current workshop, is in the process of planning a larger replacement. His country-wide contacts, provide him with many selling outlets. He also sells locally and is happy to take special orders. Bob gets great pleasure from making pots for people to use, feel and enjoy. His buoyant and gentle nature is an interesting contrast to his military background.

Anne Roper

Davanholme, Skelton, Penrith, Cumbria CA11 9SE   Map code E10
☎ 07684 84381
Open to the public by arrangement.

Anne's love of nature is apparent in her work. Seed pods, fungi, grasses and flower heads have all subconsciously influenced her delicate forms. She throws and hand-builds her pieces, most of which are then modified by pinching or the addition of texture. After drying, the pots are biscuit-fired. Washes of chrome, copper, cobalt or iron oxides are then brushed on. Some pieces have coloured glass set in them, which form pools when they fuse together in the glaze firing.

She hand-builds wall plaques with little pockets for dried grasses and also makes a vast array of miniatures. The plaques are sculpted or press-moulded in bas-relief. Her forms are unique - she lets the clay take over and the results evolve almost in spite of her. Anne uses combinations of compatible porcelain and stoneware, often modelled porcelain additions to a stoneware base. She mixes all her own glazes, the results of many tests by trial and error. Anne sometimes mixes stoneware and porcelain together, making a more easily thrown body capable of being given finely frilled edges. Pinks, greens, browns and blues feature strongly - sometimes vibrant shades, sometimes subtle and diffused. These are fired to 1280°C in an electric kiln.

Bob March:
Semi-porcellanous tableware with slip decoration,
under the stained-glass window of his porch.

⇧ *Anne Roper:*
Porcelain form with brushed oxide
decoration, on a sandstone slab in her Eden
Valley garden.

⇦ *Gosforth Pottery:*
Cobalt-decorated stoneware pots in a window
of the spacious showroom.

Anne is Cumbrian born and bred and has lived in Skelton village all her life. Skelton is a farming community with a substantial proportion of newcomers. She came to potting quite late in life; her children were all grown up. She decided to go to classes at Cumbria College of Art & Design in Carlisle, and quite by accident ended up doing pottery. She was captivated by clay and felt that she had found what she had been looking for all her life. Anne has natural ability and is largely self-taught. She has never looked back, and has set up her second pottery next to the new house that she and her husband David built in 1990. David helps with clay preparation and is very supportive. More recently, Anne has bought a gas kiln and started tests for reduction firings, which she hopes to develop.

Gosforth Pottery

Gosforth, Seascale, Cumbria CA20 1AH   Map code Co 1
☎ 09467 25296
Shop open 7 days, 10.00 to 5.30; closed Mondays from January to March

Dick and Barbara Wright sell an exceptional variety in their showroom, including the work of many other potters. This makes the shop additionally attractive to regular customers and a wonderful find for tourists and visitors. They make a wide range of reduction fired domestic stoneware that includes two standard ranges, *Cumbria Cottage*, rustic with a greeny brown glaze, and the more recent *Reflections*, reminiscent of lakes and fells. Their other popular products are three slip-cast designs in red earthenware; biscuit stamps and fish and pâté moulds. These are packaged and include recipes. They sell these in America through an agent and also here at trade and craft fairs. Many personalised items are made and commissions are also taken.

Dick and Barbara have evolved a division of labour. Dick does most of the throwing and makes the glazes. Barbara does all the decorating and calligraphy, packs the kiln and throws some garden-ware. They have an assistant for slip-casting and wedging, and another in the shop. Dick's glazes are a basic *chun* that he modifies, a blue transparent, a Cornish stone white, a greenish brown and a *tenmoku* adaptation. The stoneware is reduction-fired in a 20 cu ft propane kiln. The earthenware is fired separately in an electric kiln.

Dick began his career as a geologist, working in African gold mines. He returned to England and decided to train as a teacher, and whilst training, met Barbara. They married and, after a brief period back in Africa, they took teaching posts in Sunderland. Dick taught Geography and Barbara History. Although Dick rose to become a head of department, they both felt that teaching was not really for them. They left teaching and with friends, took over a cafe, filling station and shop close to Hadrian's Wall. This enterprise flourished, but after a while their friends decided to pull out of the partnership so the business was sold. Dick and Barbara moved to a cottage near Brampton where they decided to become potters. This may have seemed a dramatic turn of events, but Barbara had specialised in pottery at college, and Dick's geology would be an asset so they were optimistic.

They bought a wheel, and a kiln that was installed in a cow-byre. For the next two years they taught themselves the craft, drawing knowledge from whatever source they could find. They experienced numerous setbacks, but persevered, and success slowly came. They were then able to move to Gosforth and the larger premises that gave them scope for expansion. Nineteen years hard work and tenacity have rewarded them with a well-established pottery business.

Wendy Rotarides

Brentwood, Pardshaw, Cockermouth,
Cumbria CA13 0SP   Map code A5
☎ 0900 823327
By appointment only

Wendy mainly hand-builds decorative pottery using crank stoneware and porcelain clays. Some of her stoneware pots have inlays of porcelain or buff earthenware clay, giving them an ethnic African appearance. Her bottle and vase forms are coiled or slabbed, some of them having thrown necks. After adding texture, she brushes on oxides and glazes to give the matt, earthy, sometimes iridescent colours that she loves. She has a range of porcelain brooches and flower-inspired forms which she creates by rolling and pinching, and then be-jewels with fused coloured glass. Wendy mixes her own matt glazes including wood-ash, which she has evolved over many tests, and fires in an electric kiln.

Wendy's first experience with clay was at teacher's training college, where she specialised in art and crafts. Following this she taught General Subjects in a junior school, but attended evening classes in pottery and drawing at both Keswick and Cockermouth.

Coiled stoneware bottle with textured and rubbed oxide decoration

For the next few years she and her friend Chris Hawkes spent one day a week at Cumbria College of Art and Design learning ceramics. Chris and Wendy set up a pottery in the village of Pardshaw, and found many outlets for their work including Thornthwaite Gallery. Eighteen months later Chris moved away, and Wendy had to start anew. She set up her own pottery in a large Victorian house that her husband modernised.

The Guild of Lakeland Craftsmen accepted her as a member, and she was stimulated by contact with other members, which gave her more impetus. Wendy continued potting happily, almost full-time except for a little teaching at Brigham Primary School. She had a great dilemma when asked to considerably increase her teaching. Loving both potting and teaching made her choice difficult, and on this occasion she opted for teaching although she continued to pot in her spare time and maintained her outlets at Thornthwaite and Lowes Court Gallery, Egremont. In 1995 she plans to retire from teaching and is looking forward to resuming full-time potting. She considers herself very fortunate to have found two such very fulfilling careers.

Paul Scott

2 Holly Cottages, Blencogo, near Wigton, Cumbria CA7 0BZ   Map code A6
☎ 06973 61706
Not open to the public.

Paul is a ceramic artist who screen prints and paints on clay. He enjoys working with children and does many commissions and residencies in schools. He operates as a catalyst and the children produce tile panels as a joint project. The results are installed in school as a permanent record. In a recent mural, the children and staff of Upperby Primary School, Carlisle each painted a self-portrait on a tile. The subsequent whole contained 450 faces.

Paul uses T-mixture for making up frames for his screen-printed pictures which are either on paper or clay. This coarse clay is extruded forming a rebated section. It is allowed to stiffen, the corners are then mitred and cut. Using the same clay mixed to a slip, the pieces are joined. The frames dry to leather-hard, the fronts are then brushed with porcelain slip. To avoid warpage, they are dried slowly and then biscuit fired to 1000°C in an electric kiln. He next dips the slipped area into a semi-porcellaneous glaze deliberately chosen so as not to fit. The subsequent firing is to 1190°C. Crazing occurs on cooling, and he rubs Indian Ink into the cracks. After some time, more crazes form, into which he rubs a contrasting coloured ink. The results complement the prints that they frame. Paul is experimenting with other glazes such as soda or smoked sawdust firings.

The other type of clay he uses is white porcelain for his slab-built forms. Paul rolls out the clay to a thickness of approximately 3 millimetres. When leather-hard, he cuts it into components, some of which may have designs screen-printed onto them. The elements are then joined with slip to make jugs, flattened pot shapes, abstract triangular forms with corners extended. When printing, he usually prints black onto white but occasionally uses colour. The design subjects are often small everyday objects, but others are intended to make political statements. Some pieces may include simulated staples or rivets, which are brushed with metallic lustre before a third low-temperature firing.

Porcelain jug form, screen-printed with baby motifs

Paul has a BEd in Art and Design from Lancaster University. Whilst on this course he experimented with painting on clay and making up ceramic transfers. Eight years teaching in schools followed, in the middle of which he moved to Cumbria. Paul left teaching in 1985 to set up his own studio but he very much enjoys his continuing link with schools. He also writes, and as well as being a regular contributor to *Artists' Newsletter*, has started a book on clay and printing.

Dalton Pottery

8 Nelson Street, Dalton-in-Furness, Cumbria LA15 8AF   Map code S3
☎ 0229 65313
Open by arrangement

Will and Sue Thwaites work as a team and have allocated different areas of the workshop to each other. Between them they make a great variety of terracotta garden ware, some thrown and some cast. They turn out a large volume of decorative planters, from miniatures to birds, solid cast small garden gnomes and bonsai pots. They sell through garden centres, large flower shows around the country, and from their premises.

The mould-making room is definitely Will's domain. For the main part, so is the semi-industrial slip-casting room except when Sue assists with the fettling. Sue throws pots, which may be up to 10 lb. in weight, on an electric wheel, making Long Toms, basket pots, wall pots and miniature garden planters as well as small pots used as a base for dried flower arrangements. Upstairs they have another wheel where Will throws large gardenware to which they add extruded and fluted lugs. They have devised a rubber stencil which is wrapped round pots and then soft clay is pressed into the holes to create a trailing ivy design. The large ware includes strawberry pots and planters with frilled decoration.

Will has an incredible ability to improvise or invent any pieces of equipment they need. He mixes casting slip in a blunger, and adds chemicals. It is then screened through into a larger blunger below, and then pumped up through a pipe line. Will uses the pipe's nozzle to fill his plaster moulds with the slip. He built the down-draught kiln (about 60 cu ft) with the front of the kiln suspended on pulleys. The front becomes the door as it glides open or shut on its curved rails. To supplement the existing drier he has added ducts to channel surplus heat from the kiln to the mould-drying unit. The densely packed firings take from 15 to 18 hours, and the initial part of the firing has to be slow to drive off the chemically combined water through open vents.

Will and Sue originally trained as teachers at Ripon. She specialised in ceramics, and his subjects were Biology and General Science. They got married and bought a house with some outbuildings at Dalton. Will had grown up in this area, and he started to teach locally, but Sue decided that she wanted to become a potter. Will helped her set up the workshop, and gradually became more involved. With some assistance from Sue he taught himself to throw. He decided to learn about mould making and casting and went on courses during the school holidays. Will gave up teaching in the summer of 1992 to go into full-time business with Sue. He felt that slip-casting was essential to make the business viable. He has become very skilled at mould-making and uses both open-cast and the more complicated solid-cast methods. The science of slip-casting is very exacting and his knowledge in this area has helped too.

Will Thwaites filling moulds with casting slip

Pottering

Rene Roberts

Human beings hev queer ideas,
Like sailin' roond t' world in a yacht
But mine is nobbut a laal idea,
Ah'd like ter throw a pot.

Nut ter thrown yan in a temper,
Wen t' world isn't deune much good,
NO. Wat Ah want is ter MEK a pot,
Wid a dirty girt handful o' mud.

See Ah went off ter Wetheriggs Pottery
Where Ah met up wid Peter Strong,
An he show't mer hoo ter mek clart inter
    clay,
By Gow -- he knows reet frae wrong.

Ah watch 't a feller makkin' vases
Wid a perfect fluted rim,
Ah can't even deue that wid pasties
Ah never git an even rim.

Mi heed wes reelin' wid knowledge,
Wot Beehives and Pugmills can mek,
Wid Blungers an' Coo horns an' quills frae
    geese
An sagger mekker's knockers -- an' sec.

He show't mer hoo they git stacke't an' fire't
In a thoosand degree 'crematorium',
An when they war cold and patterned wid
    'slip'
Thet wer sell't in yon grand emporium.

An then we cum ter t' best bit for me,
In t' sheds wid an oppen spot
Where visitors are invited ter 'hev a go'
An try ter mek a pot.

Peter fetched mer a lump of clay
(An het watter cos t' day wes cold)
An he showed mer hoo ter kick start t' wheel
An keep t' clay in a tight hold.

Aw went weel, till Ah startit ter laff,
Then t' clay whemmled and cum alive,
An Ah cudn't hod it onter t' wheel
An it teuk a runnin' dive.

But mi secind try wes better,
Ah gat t' rhythm reet wid mi leg,
An Peter sed "Nut much like a vase,
Mair a cup for an ortrich egg!"

But -- Ah'd realised mi ambition
Which nobbut gaas ter show,
Yer nivver ower auld ter throw a pot,
OR ---- mek a pot ter THROW!

Rene Roberts is a local author of Cumbrian Dialect, and wrote these lines on her first visit to Wetheriggs Pottery in 1992.

GLOSSARY

ball clay	plastic clay from Dorset and Devon
bat	circular wooden board
bentonite	highly plastic clay mixed into glazes to keep them in suspension
biscuit-fired	low temperature first fired clay, still porous
blunger	mixer for clay and water prior to screening
body stains	commercial colourings for glazes, etc
burnish	process of polishing leather-hard clay with a spoon or pebble
Casting slip	clay mixed with de-flocculant to become a viscous liquid suitable for casting
celadon	family of reduction-fired, iron bearing glazes that produce greens
chun	stoneware glaze with an opalescent or blue-white tinge
climbing kiln	Japanese style kiln built up a hill, often with one chamber stepped above another
coil	a roll of clay
coiling	technique, building up rolls of clay by hand
comb	toothed implement passed over slip surface as decorative technique
crank	coarse clay used for hand-building; possesses low shrinkage and warpage properties
craze	cracks formed due to unequal shrinkage of clay and glaze
cross-draught	type of air circulation created in a climbing kiln
dipped	a piece immersed in glaze
dolomite	opacifier which promotes mattness in glazes
down-draught	design of kiln in which the flue exit is at the bottom
earthenware	a low firing, non-vitrified clay
enamel	coloured powders mixed with oil or turps; painted on glaze and low fired
extrude	force through a die as in a pug-mill
fabric	old-fashioned name for body clay
facets	flat sides created around a formed pot
fettling	trimming or tidying seams or imperfections before firing
fireclay	refractory clay used for firebricks, or stoneware body mix
float	process in a kiln in which the contents take up colour from a glaze component, e.g. copper, present on only some of the pots
flutes	parallel grooves cut out of pot for decoration
fly-ash	floating wood-ash in a kiln which melts at stoneware temperatures and adds a new surface dimension
foot	turned plinth or ring at base of pot; may be integral part of overall form
frit	a melt of glaze ingredients subsequently ground to a powder

grog	ground down previously fired pottery
hakeme	technique using a type of wide brush for decorating a light slip on a dark body to show brush texture
hand-built	pottery constructed by hand without the use of a potter's wheel
hump mould	a plaster former over which sheets of clay are draped
incising	cutting a design into clay using a pointed or chiselled tool
jig-and-jolley	fixed mould on a revolving wheel-head with arm and fixed profile; used for mass-production, e.g. of plant pots
kick wheel	foot operated potter's wheel
lead bisilicate	frit of lead and silica used for earthenware glazes
leather-hard	a stage in drying where clay will hold its shape
long tom	long type of flower pot specially for plants with a long tap root
lug	type of handle ("ear") added to pot
lustre	liquid preparation of metallic salts mixed with thinners and applied to glazed ware and low fired
Ochre	iron oxide
open-cast	slipcast technique using an open plaster mould
overglaze	second glaze dipped or poured over first
oxide	mineral used as a glaze ingredient producing colours which vary according to the kiln atmosphere
paper resist	paper design stuck onto leather-hard pot, then slipped and peeled off to leave an unslipped area
patinate	to give a bronze-like finish
pinched	clay hand-built using a circular motion, squeezing between finger and thumb
plastic	pliable, malleable
porcelain	white translucent high-fired clay body
press-mould	plaster mould for use with plastic clay
pug-mill	mechanical mixer of clay which extrudes
raku	(Japanese for happy) pieces are quickly fired then withdrawn with tongs into sawdust, leaves or water to quench and thereby reduce
raw glaze	a thicker glaze applied to an unfired pot, and then once-fired
reducing atmosphere	oxygen-starved atmosphere in kiln
reduction-firing	firing in a reducing atmosphere

refractory	ability to withstand extremely high temperature
rib	tool used to aid throwing and shaping
rubber kidney	tool used for smoothing clay surface

Salt glaze — sodium chloride used as a glaze; volatilises forming an "orange peel" glaze and giving off toxic fumes

scraffito	scratched decoration, often through slip
screened	passed through a sieve
sienna	ochrous earth-brownish yellow used as a pigment
slip	creamy liquid mixture of clay and water
slip glaze	glaze with a large amount of clay in the recipe
soak	to maintain maximum temperature for uniformity of firing
soda firing	common soda used instead of salt, does not produce toxic fumes
solid cast	slip cast between inner and outer plaster moulds
sponge stencil	decorative technique in which a sponge shape, soaked in slip or glaze is stamped on pot
sprig-mould	small press-mould used to create decorative addition to main pot
St Thomas' body	a type of commercial stoneware clay
stoneware	a clay which is high fired producing a vitrified body

T mixture — coarse clay used in modelling; has an open body and characteristics of low shrinkage and warpage

tenmoku	glaze with a high iron content which is reduction-fired and produces black pigment, breaking to rust
terra sigillata	fine earthenware slip used as a ground for burnishing
thrower	person who makes pots on a wheel
trail	piped decoration using a rubber bulb (or similar) filled with slip
trolley kiln	large kiln with inner shelving on rails to facilitate loading and unloading
turning	process of finishing base or shape of pot with a tool at leather-hard stage, as on a lathe

Vitrified — high fired clay with particles fused together and thereby made impervious to liquid

volatilise	evaporate, as in salt glaze or soda firing

Wax resist — process in which an area is painted with wax so as to resist glaze. Usually on base or rebate to facilitate glazing

wedge	mixing clay by hand to create even texture and remove air

Zinc oxide — glaze ingredient used as an opacifier and to obtain a matt finish

References and Further Reading

Brears P *The English Country Pottery - its history and techniques*; David and Charles, 1972

Bulmer, ed *Bulmer's Directory 1884 of East Cumberland*

Cumberland Trade Directory 1883

Draper J *Post Mediæval Pottery*; Shire Publications, Aylesbury HP17 9AJ

Fancy H *A Visit to Wilkinson's Pottery, Whitehaven 1851*; Friends of Whitehaven Museum

Haslam J *Mediæval Pottery*; Shire Publications, Aylesbury HP17 9AJ

Lawrence H *Yorkshire Pits and Potteries*; David and Charles, 1974

Ruston J H *Ruskin Pottery*; Sandwell Borough Town Hall, B70 8DX, 1990

Sibson F *The History of the West Cumberland Potteries*; Albert Chan, Hong Kong, 1991

Swan V G *Pottery in Roman Britain*; Shire Publications, Aylesbury HP17 9AJ

Weatherill L and Edwards R
Pottery Making in London and Whitehaven in the Late 17th Century; article in *Post Mediæval Archaeology*, Vol 5, 1971

White A *Burton-in-Lonsdale Country Pottery*; Lancaster University (Local Studies No. 10), 1989

MUSEUMS

Local pottery is in the collections or displays of the following establishments:

Abbot Hall Art Gallery, Kirkland, Kendal LA9 5AL. ☎ 0539 722464

Helena Thompson Museum, Park End Road, Workington CA14 4DE. ☎ 0900 62598

Keswick Museum, Station Road, Keswick CA12 4NF. ☎ 07687 73263

Penrith Museum, Robinson's School, Middlegate, Penrith CA11 7PT. ☎ 0768 64671 ext 228

The Dock Maritme Museum, North Road, Barrow-In-Furness LA14 2PW. ☎ 0229 870871

Tullie House Museum and Art Gallery, Castle Street, Carlisle CA3 8TP. ☎ 0228 34781

Wetheriggs Pottery Museum, Clifton Dykes, Penrith CA10 2DH. ☎ 0768 62946

Whitehaven Museum, Civic Hall, Lowther Street, Whitehaven CA28 7SH. ☎ 0946 67575 or 0946 693111 ext 307

Other notable collections are held at:

Museum of North Craven Life, Chapel Street, Settle, Yorkshire. ☎ 0729 822854 or 0282 695366 Contains many examples of pottery from Burton-in-Lonsdale.

City Museum and Art Gallery, Hanley, Stoke-on-Trent. ☎ 0782 202173. Holds a wonderful collection of ceramics from all periods.

VOCATIONAL COURSES IN CUMBRIA

Carlisle College of Further Education
Victoria Place, Carlisle CA1 1HS. ☎ 0228 24464
GCE A-level in Sculpture and Ceramics

Barrow-in-Furness College of Further Education
Howard Street, Barrow-in-Furness LA14 1LU. ☎ 0229 825017
BTEC First Diploma in Design
BTEC National Diploma in Design
Both courses contains elements of ceramics

Cumbria College of Art & Design
Brampton Road, Carlisle CA3 9AY. ☎ 0228 25333
HND in Design Crafts, Ceramics and Textiles; a two-year full-time course

INDEX
of Cumbrian potters and ceramic artists, 1993

EDEN CRAFT GALLERY

St Andrew's Churchyard, Penrith
Cumbria
Telephone Penrith (0768) 67955

The Eden Craft Gallery sells work by the most skilled of our local craftsmen. More than 40 crafts are on display, making this the ideal shop to buy gifts for any occasion.

Our range includes work by

Geoff & Christine Cox
Bob March
John Drinkwater
Adrian Newnham

And upstairs is

serving delicious vegetarian and wholefood dishes.
Homemade and using the finest ingredients.

Lunches & Afternoon Teas
Quality coffee and speciality tea

GOSFORTH POTTERY

Gosforth Pottery is a busy country pottery. The shop stocks pots made in the pottery and many others. During holiday times, visitors can see work in progress. Demonstrations and Have A Go are at set times - usually afternoons.
We are a National Park Information Point.

Leave the A595 at Gosforth. The pottery is at the northern end of the village, and some parking is available.

Open daily all year except:
Mondays from January to March,
25 and 26 December and 1 January

Groups accepted by appointment

POTTERY COURSES

For details of residential and day courses, and Raku evenings contact:

GOSFORTH POTTERY
GOSFORTH
WEST CUMBRIA CA20 1AH

☎ 09467 25296